ON THE ROYAL ROAD

THE
SEAGULL
LIBRARY OF
GERMAN
LITERATURE

ON THE ROYAL ROAD

THE BURGHER KING

ELFRIEDE JELINEK

TRANSLATED BY GITTA HONEGGER

LONDON NEW YORK CALCUTTA

This publication has been supported by a grant from
the Goethe-Institut India

bm:uk Austrian Federal Ministry for
Education, the Arts and Culture

The first English publication of this book was supported
by a grant from the Austrian Federal Ministry of Education,
the Arts and Culture

Seagull Books, 2022

Originally published in German as *Am Königsweg*
© Rowohlt Verlag, Reinbek bei Hamburg, 2020

First published in English translation by Seagull Books, 2020
Translation and Introduction © Gitta Honegger, 2020

ISBN 978 1 80309 230 0

British Library Cataloguing-in-Publication Data
A catalogue record for this book is available from the British Library.

Typeset by Seagull Books, Calcutta, India
Printed and bound by WordsWorth India, New Delhi, India

CONTENTS

vii

Introduction

1

ON THE ROYAL ROAD:

THE BURGHER KING

139

P.S. January 2020

143

TRANSLATOR'S UPDATE, MARCH 2020

The Coronation of King Trump

In the Beginning Was the Word

'Mad world! Mad kings! Mad composition!'

—William Shakespeare, *King John*, Act 2, Scene 1

'Here he is!, the King, everything has happened already, but isn't over yet. Or will it only begin to happen, or is it currently happening elsewhere, in another dimension?'

—Elfriede Jelinek, *On the Royal Road*: *The Burgher King*

Donald Trump was elected President of the United States on Tuesday, November 8, 2016. One day short of three weeks later, on Monday, December 2016, Nobel laureate Elfriede Jelinek mailed the first draft of her play *Am Königsweg* (*On the Royal Road*), her stunningly prescient response to that fateful day, to her editor, Nils Tabert, the head of Rowohlt Verlag's theatre publications. She submitted the revised version on January 9, 2017. On March 27,

2017, the world premiere of a staged reading of an abbreviated English version in my translation, now titled *On the Royal Road: The Burgher King* was presented in New York City at the Martin E. Segal Theatre Center, 21 blocks south of the Trump Towers. The award-winning world premiere of the full German text followed on October 28, 2017 at the Schauspielhaus Hamburg, directed by Falk Richter. The play was one of the most produced works in the German-language theater during the following season.

When I started to write this introduction, Speaker of the United States House of Representatives, Nancy Pelosi, had just announced the formal impeachment inquiry about President Trump.[1] It was the House Democrats' response to an anonymous whistleblower's bombshell report about a troubling telephone conversation between Trump and Ukrainian president, Volodymyr Zelinsky. Allegedly, Trump pressured the fledgling president to investigate former vice president Joseph Biden's son for corruption as a board member of the Ukrainian gas company Burisma during his father's vice-presidency. Quite obviously, Trump's primary target was (and continues to be) the elder Biden, a leading presidential candidate and Trump's perceived foremost political rival, who, he insinuated, might have tried to facilitate his son's business dealings in the Ukraine during his vice-presidency. As I was writing this, NBC breaking news popped up on my computer with the announcement that the White House accidentally sent an e-mail, meant for its allies, suggesting talking points to counter arguments from House

---

1 September 25, 2019.

Democrats, to House Democrats including Nancy Pelosi. It took an actor, John Lithgow, to cut to the chase of this absurd scenario in a *New York Times* op-ed, titled: "Trump is a Bad President. He is an Even Worse Entertainer. The performer in chief is forcing us to live in a B-horror movie." In his perceptive commentary, the 2-time Oscar nominee wryly sums up the transcontinental presidential exchange: "In recent weeks, we've even read about our ex-reality-show-host president discussing foreign policy over the phone with the ex-TV comedian president of Ukraine."[2]

Under these circumstances, it stands to reason, as much as there is left in this out-of-joint world, that it is late-night stand-up comedians, such as Stephen Colbert, Seth Myers, or ("Trump could be the first American president to get impeached by a whistleblowjob") Jimmy Kimmel, who are Trump's most astute, sharp-shooting critics at the same time as they are urgent bedtime therapy for their audiences. How else to process the president's tweet after he had more or less given President Erdogan of Turkey—in a telephone conversation—the green light to invade Syria in the latter's genocidal pursuit of the Kurds: "As I have stated strongly before, and just to reiterate, if Turkey does anything that I, *in my great and unmatched wisdom*, consider to be off limits, *I will totally destroy and obliterate the Economy of Turkey (I've done before!)*" [emphasis added].[3] "Is It a Comedy? Is It

---

2 Available at: https://nyti.ms/2ICLR8w (last accessed on March 10, 2020).

3 Donald Trump (@realDonaldTrump). Twitter, October 7, 2019. Available at: http://bit.ly/39DDbLd (last accessed on March 10, 2020).

a Tragedy?" is the title of a short story by the late Austrian writer Thomas Bernhard to whom Jelinek is frequently compared in terms of their acid humor and stinging criticism of their country. In the case of Jelinek's unnamed king, it is a farcicatastrophical global political reality show. In very different styles, both Jelinek and Bernhard are controversial path- and taboo-breakers in post–World War II Western "serious" literature at the same time as they are profoundly over-the-top comedians of culture.

Nevertheless, as the events continue to unfold at breakneck speed and with, as of now, unstoppable tragic consequences, how could the theatre or any fictionalized account of the 45th American president's mafia-style leadership catch up with the bizarre twists and turns of events, let alone be taken seriously. How would this text, authored by an outsider, a foreigner to boot, hold up more than two and a half years into his tumultuous presidency? Moreover, by the time this volume will be published, the presidential campaign will be in full swing, if not already decided.

Jelinek is no stranger to instant dramatic interventions in acute political crises. Since she received the Nobel Prize in 2004, most of her many performance texts are intense responses to current events, from the 2008 global financial crisis, the treatment of migrants, to the *Charlie Hebdo* massacre in Paris.[4] But she is not interested in chronicling, "dramatizing" the real-life dramas or tragedies. Her complex, often darkly vaudevillian attacks on contemporary society

---

4 *Fury* (*Wut*), published in my translation by Seagull Books, 2022.

are filtered through the lenses of history, philosophy, literature, drama, and significantly, the media, gossip columns, and popular culture. The issues transcend the specifics of time, place, and contemporary figures, and gain universal resonances. As one German critic suggested with regard to the play: "Once, when the 45th US president will be history, this history play might well be read as we read Shakespeare's *Richard III*. The topical references will have been lost. Jelinek's captivating thoughts about power, delusionary blindness and hubris will hold their universality."[5]

Jelinek's easily recognizable King remains unnamed throughout. With uncanny foresight, she introduces a blind seer, her appropriation of Tiresias, as the main speaker. To an extent, Jelinek might even have foreseen her own blindness inasmuch as she assumed that Trump would not remain president for long. Her strong trust in and concern about US democracy is a legacy of its role as an important model after World War II. But she accurately diagnosed Trump's laziness, which only much later was revealed in the Special Council investigation. Her seer is a woman bleeding from the eyes and with the features of Miss Piggy, the beloved, outrageous character from the legendary *Muppet Show*. This iconic figure firmly roots the text in the US, but she also serves as a medium for the author herself, an outsider, a foreigner, through the looking glass. And what she finds there

---

5 Quoted by Bärbel Lücke, "Blindness Without Insight. Eine sprachanalytische Untersuchung zu Elfriede Jelineks Am Königsweg" in Elfriede Jelinek, *Forschungsjahrbuch 2018/19* (Pia Janke ed.) (Vienna: Praesens Verlag, 2019), pp. 29–53.

is a world where everything is, if not totally reversed, completely out of joint. The unnamed elephant in the room is refracted through Greek mythology, most prominently the blinded Oedipus Tyrannos; the Muppets; Paul Girard, the philosopher, best known for his book *Violence and the Sacred*; David Graeber, the anthropologist and author of *Debt*; Sigmund Freud; David Cay Johnston, the Trump biographer;[6] the media; and, as always, Martin Heidegger.

This is the first time that Jelinek introduces the German philosopher by name. If the prospective theater producer is wondering what light this controversial—for most of us unintelligible—thinker could possibly shed on Trump and stops reading right here, may they be reminded that, at the time of the Nazis' rise, Heidegger, the philosophical genius, let himself be blinded by the Führer, and naively thought that he, the thinker, could lead the leader. And, perhaps not surprisingly, some of his thoughts are directly applicable to the world we live in now:

> Someone is acting "politically" in the modern sense who, e.g., obtains the payment promised, though at first withheld, for betraying another country and obtains it specifically by utilizing the friendly mediation of the very country he betrayed. Politics [*Politik*] no longer has anything to do with the *polis*, ["city-state"] nor with morals and least of all with "becoming a people." In the age of complete de-divinization, politics is the only appropriate basic

6 David Cay Johnston, *The Making of Donald Trump* (London: Melville House, 2016).

form of the forceful gathering of all means of power and ways of violence, i.e. the only form that acknowledges the authority of no court of law and derives everything legitimate from "rights," i.e. from the power to claim "life," i.e. from the empowerment of power, indeed such that the talk of "rights" is tolerated only as a vestige of overcome notions of order, so as to re-accustom into the new order those who are ponderous and laden with old prejudices.[7]

How ironic in view of Heidegger's early sympathy for Hitler that his ponderings on power and violence, on a "new order that is laden with old prejudices," at the height of World War II ring true even today. And beyond "ironic" that he does it in the context of his anti-semitism which comes up throughout the notebooks and which he never publically acknowledged.[8]

Note, for example, his thoughts on race:

That the age of machination elevates race to the explicit and expressly instituted "principle of history" (or only of historiology) is not the arbitrary invention of "doctrinaire" individuals, but is instead a *consequence* which must subjugate beings, in all

---

7 Martin Heidegger, *Ponderings XII–XV: Black Notebooks 1939–1941* (Richard Rojcewicz trans.) (Bloomington: Indiana University Press, 2017), p. 34, Section 22.

8 Jelinek wrote a play about a fictitious meeting between Heidegger and Hanna Arendt after World War II. See Elfriede Jelinek, "Totenauberg. (Death/Valley/Summit)" in Carl Weber (ed.), *DramaContemporary: Germany* (Baltimore, MD: Johns Hopkins University Press, 1996), pp. 217–63.

their domains, to planning and calculation. Racial thinking makes "life" a form of breeding which is a kind of calculation. *With their emphatically calculative giftedness*, the Jews have for the longest time been "living" in accord with the principle of race, which is why they are offering the most vehement resistance to its unrestricted application. The instituting of racial breeding stems not from "life" itself, but from the overpowering of life by machination.[9]

"Calculation" and "machination" are, of course, age-old stereotypical qualities attributed to the Jews.

And Jelinek never tires to—in her words—make an ass out of the thinker and, in the same breath, apparently of herself. In the words of Miss Piggy: "Herr Heidegger is to blame, for once I am addressing him personally now, because many times he has served me well, inasmuch as I misunderstood him: What's got in your mind, no one else would have gotten? I don't yet even understand what I could misunderstand."[10]

If the author's self-mockery is endearingly encouraging to the uninitiated reader, it is also somewhat disingenuous: there is, after all, method in her "misunderstanding." To get to that very clear self-assessment, she had to have learned a lot from Heidegger. But it takes a brilliant intuitive intelligence—an artist's understanding of language—to absorb in order to then twist his convoluted investigations of word roots into

---

9 Heidegger, *Ponderings XII–XV*, p. 44, Section 83.

10 See p. 53.

apparently utter nonsense. The German idiom for such twisting describes Jelinek's strategy much better: "to churn somebody's (every) word in his mouth." The nonsense that foams out in a cascade of speech-bubbles conveys the traumatizing madness of the dictatorial regime that would, in Miss Piggy's prophetic vision, befall the shell-shocked nation and, in its wake, the world. Jelinek's mangled Heidegger-speak echoes the wisdom of the Shakespearean Fool.

Most of her work, haunted by the legacy of history, especially the Holocaust, is peopled by the Undead inhabiting the living; her unnamed living ruler is co-inhabited by several. The play's bracketed opening lines suggest a search for those Undead, an author in search of characters: (Vespasian? Cola di Rienzi?). She quickly drops the thought of Medea, though, and suggests herself in the female puppet figure of the seer. The blood, coming from Miss Piggy's/the authors eyes, is also a general mark of gender as frequently mocked by the president-elect.

Autographical snippets are strewn throughout the text, such as mundane (thus universal) conflicts with the neighbor about the spreading of dandelion from his garden. Girard places neighborly conflicts at the core of the violence ritualized in the sacrifices of ancient cultures, and sees them continued in the significance of the scapegoat or the victim, as Trump sees himself vis-à-vis his opponents. Playing off Girard's elaborations on violence and the sacred, Jelinek even anticipates Trump's recent self-identification as the savior, specifically of Israel. "Trump Declares Himself 'King' of Israel—the Second Coming of God"[11] reads the headline in *Vanity Fair*. "Trump Declares Himself the Chosen One," announces *The Times of Israel*, two and a half years after Jelinek had finished her text.[12]

Girard speaks of the scapegoat as the reconciling victim who reunites a society in conflict, with Oedipus as the archetypal example. In Jelinek's variation on the theme, the nameless elephant as God and King victimizes everyone, but is insatiable: no sacrifice, no sacrificial victim could ever reconcile him. In real life, in the third year of the presidential reality show, the president has styled himself as the supreme, the one and only victim. The victim, no less, of a lynching, as he declared with utter disregard of the term's painful and shameful historical resonances in the US: "Trump as Victim. Trump's Political Defense: Play the Victim Card."[13] "The Horrendous Message Behind Trump's Lynching Tweet."[14]

In Jelinek's twisting of Girard's terminology, Trump could be the—in his terminology, PERFECT—reconciling

11 Bess Levin, "Trump Declares Himself 'King of Isreal,' the 'Second Coming of God,'" *Vanity Fair*, August 21, 2019. Available at: http://bit.ly/-3aFAGrH (last accessed on March 10, 2020).

12 *Times of Israel*, "Trump Declares Himself to Be 'the Chosen One,'" *Times of Israel*, August 22, 2019. Available at: http://bit.ly/2xkFvZ7 (last accessed on March 10, 2020).

13 Gabby Orr and Daniel Lippman, "Trump's Political Defense: Play the Victim Card," *Politico*, September 26, 2019. Available at: https://-politi.co/39yTVDj (last accessed on March 10, 2020).

14 Jason Morgan Ward, "The Horrendous Message behind Trump's 'Lynching' Tweet." CNN, October 23, 2019. Available at: https://cnn.it/-2TVRtQR (last accessed on March 10, 2020).

victim who might unite the warring parties in nothing but their apparent irreconcilability. Miss Piggy saw it coming:

> Old resentments, old hatred—which should actually be spread out among all of you, so everyone can get something out of them, says this man—are directed at one single individual, [. . .] they are directed at the King who everyone could be, but is not, you didn't know that, huh? The King is he, it's him alright, and now he should be the one everything flows into, hopes first, they'll soon be checked off, but the feelings of hate, resentment, how about those? Directed at him, the King, the one and only, the reconciling sacrifice.[15]

The Oedipus myth provides the overarching theme of blindness, with violence—it's seeds spread by the gods' oracles generate involuntary patricide and incest, suicide and self-immolation—the leitmotif, all of which are also rooted in our existential blindness. A blindness ultimately toward ourselves, our need for gods we invented as justification for our violence and its punishment. The Old Testament's "eye for an eye" is Trump's favorite motto, as he declared during his first presidential campaign.[16] But Miss Piggy–Jelinek's eyes are open wide. Her self-anointed godly King derives his traits from the old-testamentary God the Father, as well as from Abraham, the chosen human father, ordered by the

---

15 See p. 136.

16 Nolan D. Mccaskill, "Trump's Favorite Bible Verse: 'Eye for an Eye,'" *Politico*, April 14, 2016. Available at: https://politi.co/2vVgdAt (last accessed on March 10, 2020).

Almighty to kill his son Isaac as proof of his loyalty. The same god will eventually sacrifice his miraculously begotten son.

Tracing the American king's blindness further back to Oedipus, the son, incestuous husband, and father in one, Jelinek hints at Trump's Freudian bond with his daughter. For a brief moment, the daughters of Oedipus are brought into the picture, nameless and hardly recognizable. Fleetingly, Jelinek casts herself as Antigone and, as such, advises herself (through Miss Piggy) to get over her writerly obsession with Trump, a madly self-destructive father/authority complex:

> Hey, you must have a complex regarding this man, regarding any man! Get over it, get with it. Your complex must be dropped, because the time of dissolution has come. You should quickly dissolve your complex, or you'll become unhappy, pregnant with doom as you always are. You are not a savior, you are not one who talks but one who writes, it is quieter, makes less noise, okay, have it your way, there is no one, literally no one who listens, they are listening to someone else. You and your kind are no longer important, go ahead, wait till you are blue in the face, but nothing will happen. You must follow the sister, who will guide you not like a blind king, follow you must, albeit unwillingly.[17]

Channeled by Miss Piggy, Jelinek's characters and herself bleed into each other. Identifying with Antigone triggers

---

17 See p. 80.

a recollection of her relationship with her own father, veiled, nonetheless, by a Freudian fairy tale haunted by ancient myths and rituals and revived in an American nightmare:

> The little girl who wanted to think of herself as the father's favorite lover, had to experience a hard punishment by her father, she spilled hot tea over the night table that was more valuable than she and more valuable than the father, otherwise he wouldn't have had to hit hard, truth be told, Mr. King, yes you, the heavy hitter who just won the bid, in truth?, and so for the girl the sky is falling.[18]

Violence, religion, and money are intricately connected in David Graeber's internationally acclaimed book *Debt: The First 5,000 Years*. Intrigued by the continued moral power of debt, Graebner traces its history back to the earliest Vedic poems which treat debt as synonymous with guilt and sin.[19] Owing their lives to the gods and their royal descendants, to parents, teachers, society, and to humanity as a whole, humans are born into debt and thus obligated to continuously pay back, through sacrifices of various kinds, and eventually in taxes to the state. Failure to do so is punished or revenged with violence. Trump's obsessive use or threat of sanctions in international politics is the global application of such punishment, with catastrophic consequences, as evidenced in his betrayal of Turkey's Kurdish minority in October 2019, or his friendship with Saudi Arabia and the US

---

18 See pp. 81–2.

19 David Graebner, *Debt: The First 5,000 Years* (London: Melville House, 2014), p. 56.

military backing of its gruesome intervention in Yemen's civil war. If in the Vedic tradition the debt of humans is owed to death and they pay it back with their lives, Trump's foreign policies are in the service of Death. The seeds for his actions are already suggested in Jelinek's unique composite of the ruler.

Like in all Indo-European languages, the German term for debt and guilt/sin is the same: *Schuld* (*Ich bin in Deiner Schuld*: I am indebted to you, I owe you something). True to her games with language, Jelinek plays with countless variations of this complex double meaning; it has become a constant in many of her works. Since the commonly used English version departed from King James version's "Father, forgive us our debts as we forgive our debtors, to "forgive us our sins, as we forgive others who sin against us," the double resonances are more or less lost to or forgotten by the contemporary worshipper or reader. (The interaction of *Schuld* as guilt and debt in the financial sense poses an ongoing challenge for this translator not only in in many Jelinek texts.)

Trump, on the other hand, never guilty of anything but always the victim, has a clear-cut interpretation of the Christian belief: that debts should be forgiven (in his case, most of all, forgotten) when it comes to *his* unpaid debts, but severely punished if perceived as owed to him. Having established himself as "l'État C'èst Moi," he extends his God-given right of punishment to US foreign aid, trade, and other international agreements, and on the domestic front, of demanding his version of reconciling sacrifices from his subjects which are doomed to never be enough. This is what Girard's theory of the sacrifice in crisis has come down to in Jelinek's subversion of the ruler's perverted world-view, which earned him, among many others, the title of "Clown-in-Chief."

Following Jelinek's ruminations about the biblical God-Father's shockingly cruel demand from Abraham (perhaps crueler, as it turns out to have been a test only), in the context of Jelinek's other fathers, including her own (and, not to forget Oedipus's father abandoning his infant son), HE could be considered the original progenitor of the violence his commands have set off throughout history. But ultimately, Jelinek's complex elaboration of the sacrificial victim's identity must lead one to the conclusion that it was humans who needed to invent their gods in order to justify their violence and punish that of others. Faith is the existential blindness of believers, as evidenced in Abraham's readiness to commit filicide, the ultimate act of violence. In return for the sacrifice of Isaac, God promised Abraham that his descendants would inherit the land of Israel. In view of God's horrifying demand, Jelinek tosses out the provocative question: Can Abraham (in his blind faith?), rather than Isaac, be considered the sacrificial victim? Jelinek's associative method challenges, even invites, her readers, theatre artists, translators, and audiences to become her collaborators by continuing the associative process on their own. Taking off from her web of associations across myth and history, God's promise of the future power of Abraham's line could be read as the foreshadowing of Satan's temptation of Christ. As a test of the Son of God's attitude toward his father, it might even have been ordered by the latter.

Thomas Aquinas cites Sirach 2: "Son, when thou comest to the service of God, stand in justice and in fear, and prepare your soul for temptation."[20] In Jelinek's appropriation of Girard's analysis of the sacrificial victim's function, it becomes the foundational principle of all religions. The exchange value of power is human life. Fast-forward to Jelinek's view of Abraham and Isaac through the prism of the market's current mythical power (and its blinding effects). Though not acknowledged as a source, Karl Marx comes into play in Jelinek's staging of the workers as sacrificial victims of the market due to the outsourcing of production, the death of their class materialized in the abandoned factories and mines, with the biblical Isaac as the archetype for their endangerment.

The iconic figure of Abraham remains an enigma as both victim of divine psycho-terror and willing executioner of the Word of God, or rather, simply, in all its ambiguity, just "The Word." Whether sacred or profane, revealed truth or the truth of fiction, it is the writer's precious, much-abused, maligned, and embattled tool. Her "employee," her worker, as Jelinek, the ultimately impotent writer ironically sets herself apart from the betrayed real workers:

---

20 Quoted in Matt Emerson, "Why Did Christ Allow Himself to Be Tempted?" *America: The Jesuit Review*, February 23, 2015. Available at: http://bit.ly/2TQC6Jj (last accessed on March 10, 2020).

I am self-employed, mostly manually, but don't know where my hands should go. I speak, therefore I also employ words whom I pay nothing but my attention. Call it minimum job security, without the security as to how it will go, which will be the next word to make sense, none of them have any. They are superfluous. My, our words are superfluous. The other words are talking now, they say something entirely different.[21]

At the end of her (wordy) text, the writer has, that is, writes, speaks the last word, whoever her staged stand-in may be:

There is nothing there, only desolation. No factories. No mines. No work. No works. Someone spoke to us, we did not hear it, but someone must have said it: Away with it, away with the word, with every word, we'd rather pick a different word, so that we can lose it too, we lost everything, now we are also running out of words, they are running off to where there still is room for conversation. Please take your place on the sacrificial rock, make yourself comfortable, I am just getting the knife: Abraham! Abraham! And he answers, as said before, not by me, so it is correct: I am here. Just a moment I can't see exactly who that even is, but he seems to be here. My word has gone crazy, probably because it thought it lost me, but I am not at a loss for words and the word

---

21 See pp. 130.

speaks: Do not lay your hand on the boy or do anything to him, for now I know that you fear God, seeing you have not withheld your son, your only son, for my sake![22]

The ending opens a Pandora's box of questions: Who is it that first spoke this story? What/who was the word that was in the beginning? Does Isaac stand for the word as the sacrificial victim signaling the imminent ending of the word as we understood it and misunderstood it in our endless search for truth, that keeps us going? Isaac's death is averted at the last moment. Can the word still maintain a ray of hope amid the disfiguring, deadly violence of power? As far as this play goes, the rest is silence.

Readers, performers, directors, be advised: Don't get stuck trying to figure out the linear logic of an individual sentence (let the dramaturgs do that). Rather, follow the— often long—trails of word games and puns, jump from root to root like over stones across a river while the words stream by, trace the texture of the text, and the pictures in her "planes of language," her "word-scapes," will come together like a jigsaw puzzle.

Or read the text aloud, like a musical score. Be sure to follow her punctuations, and you will hear the tone of voice, the specific rhetoric of her figures and get the rhythm, that carries the meaning, pick up the sound of syllables, of compound words, alliterations, discover the leitmotifs and variations.

---

22 See p. 137.

Scientist Professor Manfred Laubichler (full disclosure, my husband) found and tried to explain to me in many conversations the algorithmic structures behind it all.

Specifically, Jelinek's performance text is a mono- dialog between herself and the American president. But, as mentioned above, once all the mega-public personae alluded to fade out of memory, the author/blind seer/Miss Piggy will simply become the Writer, in the deepest sense a "Figure of Speech," struggling for the survival of the word (and truth) against its deadly abuse by power. Arguably, this is Jelinek's most personal *and* most universal text. In the face of money and power, it is a deeply disturbing testimony to the Writer's Last Stand. The seer's warning of the end of the WOR[L]D.

In that spirit, a word about the translator's challenges to do justice to Jelinek's way with words. When this becomes well-nigh impossible, the reader will find her taking a Time Out for the translator's internal dialog with "her" author. She takes this liberty with Jelinek's permission, since she also stages and generally, as well as generously, considers her translator her co-author. These inserts can be easily cut for a production. In the printed text, they can be read in lieu of footnotes, which seems awkward in a text for performance.

The Translator's Tale

For the most entertaining and astute introduction to the translator's challenges of Jelinek's linguistic strategies, I refer the reader to Mark Twain's chapter "The Awful German Language" in his book, *A Tramp Abroad*. (As I first typed the latter title, an obvious typo—a Jelinek bug?—the unnamed ruler's name slipped into the title of Twain's book.) The following is a quote from the chapter. I quote it at length, because it goes straight to the heart of her critical, satirical use of the ambiguities in a single German word:

> There are some exceedingly useful words in this lan- guage. *Schlag*, for example; and *Zug*. There are three- quarters of a column of *Schlags* in the dictionary, and a column and a half of *Zugs*. The word *Schlag* means Blow, Stroke, Dash, Hit, Shock, Clap, Slap, Time, Bar, Coin, Stamp, Kind, Sort, Manner, Way, Apoplexy, Wood-cutting, Enclosure, Field, Forest- clearing. This is its simple and *exact* meaning—that is to say, its restricted, its fettered meaning; but there are ways by which you can set it free, so that it can soar away, as on the wings of the morning, and never be at rest. You can hang any word you please to its tail, and make it mean anything you want to. You can begin with *Schlag-ader*, which means artery, and you can hang on the whole dictionary, word by word, clear through the alphabet to *Schlag-wasser*, which means bilge-water—and including *Schlag- mutter*, which means mother-in-law.[23]

For laughs, perhaps at those who think they know German and might not get the joke, Twain offers his witty, albeit sexist interpretation of *Schlagmutter* (literally, "hit- mother"), the German term for stop-nut. It is a striking

---

23 Mark Twain, *A Tramp Abroad; Following the Equator; Other Travels* (New York: Library of America, 2010), p. 383, emphases added.

(*schlagendes*) example of Jelinek's hilarious, over-the-top and somewhat hidden plays on words. Her text proves Twain's claim regarding the wide-ranging usefulness of *Schlag*, both as noun and verb (*schlagen*—to beat). In various combinations and variations, she teases 15+ wordgames out of it.

As Jelinek's fellow Viennese and as an aside for the sake of completeness, let me add *Schlagobers*, whipped cream, or *Schlag* for short, in Viennese German. Overlooked by both authors, the Viennese perceive their beloved fluffy concoction as the only authentically historical one, the crowning on their coffee and sweets. Miss Piggy would certainly pig out on it. Critics of the Viennese's fabled sweetness see it as an apt metonym for the kitschification of local culture and the sickening hypocrisy in all that sugary charm.

Now a few samples of Jelinek's diversifications of *Schlag* and the translator's woes. Already the first paragraph offers a perfect introduction to both:

> Der König sieht mir nicht danach aus, als würde er überhaupt irgendwas tun wollen. Außer Schulden machen, daran sind aber auch wir schuld. Er hat sich Geld geliehen in der Gewißheit, daß er es mit einem *Abschlag* zurückzahlen wird. Der *Abschlag* wird ein neues Loch aufreißen. Er ist mit den Schulden sehr gut gefahren, sagt er. Natürlich war er ein Drauf-gänger, aber es hat sich für ihn ausgezahlt, es war gut für ihn.[24]

24 Elfriede Jelinek, *Am Königsweg* (Hamburg: Rowohlt Theater Verlag, 2020), p. 73.

Let's start with a literal translation of this passage:

> The King doesn't look to me as if he wanted to do anything at all. Except contract debts but that's also on our account. He borrowed money, secure in the knowledge that he will repay it with a discount. The discount will tear open the next hole. Debts got him very far, he says. Of course, he was a go-getter, it paid off, he made a few killings.

My translation:

> The King doesn't look to me as if he wanted to do anything at all. Other than default, but that is surely our fault as well. He borrowed money knowing that he will pay, no play his debts to a tee. The tee gets him to the next hole. Debts got him very far. Of course, he was a daredevil, it paid off, he made a few killings.[25]

First the promising news: the English translation of *Abschlag* offers meanings that establish an additional allusion to Trump beyond the obvious financial connections:[26]

> Deduction, punt (football, rugby, etc.), tee (golf), drive (golf), markdown (discount), reduction (in price); haircut (financial loss), kick out (goal keeper), (lithic), flake, anticipated payment, pay on account, partial payment. (Needless to say, "haircut"

---

25 See p. 4.

26 See English–German Dictionary. Available at: http://bit.ly/2TQClUJ (last accessed on March 10, 2020).

is a glorious no-brainer for further punning on the King, which follows later in the play.)

Now the complications: Jelinek uses the same word *Abschlag* (in the sense of reduction in price, partial payment) twice. This would also work with the English "deduction." However—the second *Abschlag,* while continuing the monetary meaning, contains in its etymological root *schlag* the verb *schlagen.* Google offers three words, *beat, hit, strike,* each branching out into its own subset of meanings in German, depending on the context. Translating them back into English, this is what happens:

— *Beat* mutates into: hit, defeat, surpass, beat up, outdo, overbid, outpace, one-up, break the record, to be a hard act to follow.

— *Hit* can also mean to hoe, cut, carve, bash up, pound out, shoot; it can also drag in crack open with another subset of meanings.

— *Strike* adds *zuschlagen* for shut, close, nail shut, and more. Yours truly can pitch in with "go for it."

You get the picture of confusion and possible double-entendres that Jelinek can feed on; and how the translator can be misled into multiple detours that turn out to be deadends. As an example: this translator was distracted by Dict.com, which pointed out the German idiom, *Brücken schlagen.* Amid an array of synonyms for "hitting," it does not mean hitting but quite the opposite: "building bridges."[27]

---

27 See English–German Dictionary. Available at: http://bit.ly/2Q0Ejkk (last accessed on March 10, 2020).

Cynics might see this as an indication of the difference between Teutonic and Anglo methods of establishing connections. Unfortunately, there is nothing to be done with this find in this place of the text. So the translator added it to her Jelinek vocabulary for possible future use, and got back to the business at hand.

Luckily, *Abschlag* and *schlagen* are also golfing terms. We all know only too well what golf means to America's Commander-in-Cheat. (Compliments to Rick Reilly for his book with this title on the subject of presidential golf.)[28] This opens up an unexpected line of word-games pertinent to the Unnamed:

> He borrowed money knowing that he will pay, no play his debts to a tee. The tee gets him to the next hole. Debts got him very far, he says. Of course, he was a go-getter, it paid off, he made a few killings.[29]

This new word-play must compensate for the loss of Jelinek's original, playing on the double meaning of *Schuld* as both debt and guilt.

Following up on the golfing terminology somewhat shifts the emphasis of "tearing up a new hole," to the digging of a new construction site thanks to the Unnamed's machinations to repay, if at all, only a part of his debts; it is also an only tongue-in-cheek reference to his shameless perception and use of the female body. The suggestive holes in

---

28 Rick Riley, *Commander in Cheat: How Golf Explains Trump* (New York: Hachette, 2019).

29 See p. 4.

the golf-course remain rather in the realm of the a sopho-moric dirty joke which, nevertheless, is never below our ruler's limited vocabulary. Google pulls me further down with: "What Is the Size of a Golf Ball Hole." Jelinek would certainly have a ball with that one. The reader might think that "honi soit qui mal y pense." It is a tendency common to Jelinek translators to suspect an obscene subtext even where none was intended. What should at least be clear by now is that getting into the vortex of Jelinek's chains of pos-sible associations can turn into an unending exponential roller-coaster.

If the reader is still holding on to some reason (keep in mind, the subject is a totally unreasonable individual and the world around him, foreseen by Ms. Jelinek/Piggy, is out of joint), then here is a totally different, much stickier example of Jelinek's linguistic strategies:

> If you want to *stick it* to him, you must buy an *enve-lope* that really *sticks* together and *lick it* and send it or don't. (You have the choice. You don't even get near the angel, if you don't want to co-determine the fate of your country.) Go ahead, take this Cheeto Caesar, he is quite *sticky*, though you may be the one to get *licked*.[30]

> (Wenn Sie ihm eine *kleben* wollen, müssen Sie einen Briefumschlag kaufen, der auch wirklich *klebt*, und ihn *abschlecken* und *abschicken* oder auch nicht, [Sie haben die Wahl, und dem Engel kommen Sie dann

30 See pp. 48.

nicht mal in die Nähe, wenn Sie das *Geschick* Ihres
Landes nicht mitbestimmen wollen.] Nehmen Sie
doch diesen Herrscher, der ist *geschickt*, wenn auch
nicht vom Himmel.)[31]

The sentence starts: "If you want to punch him . . ." The
German *kleben* is a (lesser-used) vernacular synonym for
schlagen. Jelinek, however, takes it into a dizzying play of silly
double-entendres that reflect the rapidly increasing global
awareness of Trump's dangerous mental imbalances. The
"him" refers to a previous reference to Paul Klee's painting
Angelus Novus, famously analyzed by the philosopher Walter
Benjamin as the backward-turned "Angel of History":

[A]n angel looking as though he is about to move
away from something he is fixedly contemplating.
His eyes are staring, his mouth is open, his wings
are spread. This is how one pictures the angel of history. His face is turned toward the past. Where we
perceive a chain of events, he sees one single catastrophe, which keeps piling wreckage upon wreckage and hurls it in front of his feet. The angel would
like to stay, awaken the dead, and make whole what
has been smashed. But a storm is blowing from
Paradise; it has got caught in his wings with such
violence that the angel can no longer close them.
The storm irresistibly propels him into the future
to which his back is turned, while the pile of debris

---

31 Jelinek, *Am Königsweg*, p. 21.

before him grows skyward. This storm is what we call progress.[32]

Miss Piggy/Jelinek says that the blind seers have to constantly turn backwards, like the Angel of History, because they don't know where to look:

> [Y]es, indeed, the King's victory is the best news in centuries, well, let's say, in some time, where did he go now, the ruler? We can't find him at the moment, but we find him terrific. Just a few more steps and you'll see the future for the blind, there it is, we didn't even have to look so carefully, we would have seen it right away! The one for seers is always behind them, because it is hard for the seers to orientate themselves, therefore they don't know where in front is.[33]

Always ready to mock herself, Jelinek adds: "[The blind seers] have to turn around constantly, which does not help them, like the Angel of History, whom I drag in every time I can't think of anything else."[34]

So then, let us look again at this passage:

> Wenn Sie ihm eine *kleben* wollen, müssen Sie einen Briefumschlag kaufen, der auch wirklich *klebt*, und ihn *abschlecken* und *abschicken* oder auch nicht, [Sie haben die Wahl, und dem Engel kommen Sie dann

---

32 Wikipedia entry on *Angelus Novus*. Available at: http://bit.ly/2Q3L3Oh (last accessed on March 10, 2020).

33 See p. 47.

34 See p. 48.

nicht mal in die Nähe, wenn Sie das *Geschick* Ihres
Landes nicht mitbestimmen wollen.] Nehmen Sie
doch diesen Herrscher, der ist *geschickt*, wenn auch
nicht vom Himmel.[35]

The translator is already somewhat puzzled about *kleben*.
The first meaning that comes to mind is "stick," rather
than "punch," but what about it? Why here, why now? The
second sub-clause, which, at first glance, seems like a non-
sequitur, explains why she needs "stick." It is, because she
introduces the context of mailing a letter: " . . . you must buy
an *envelope* that really *sticks* together *and lick it* and send it
or don't."[36]

But beware, now more double-entendres are kept in
play.

Knowing Jelinek's predilection for obscenities (to reflect
the obscenities of power play) and the anonymous ruler's
obscene ways in every respect, words like licking and
sticking support such subtextual suggestions, and this translator is rewarded in the end with the punchline derived from
"licked":

Go ahead, take this Cheat-o Caesar, he is quite
sticky, though you may be the one to get licked.[37]

Still elated about her luck with lick, the translator takes
another liberty: while Jelinek speaks of "the ruler," the translator, searching for our ruler's many nicknames found

35 Jelinek, *Am Königsweg*, p. 21.

36 Jelinek, *Am Königsweg*, p. 21.

37 Jelinek, *Am Königsweg*, p. 21.

"Cheeto Ceasar" and could not resist turning it into Cheat-o Caesar (with the author's enthusiastic approval of cheapo puns). But, alas, a major stumbling block follows right after in the next sentence, which at first sight looks harmless enough:

> Nehmen Sie doch diesen Herrscher, der ist *geschickt*, wenn auch nicht vom Himmel.

> Go ahead, take this ruler, he *has been sent*, albeit not from God.[38]

Waiting in ambush once again is *geschickt*. On the one hand, it contains the verb *schicken* that fits into the context of mailing, dispatching, but as an adjective in this sub-clause, it shifts its meaning to "skilled." Depending on the tone of voice, it communicates a sardonic "he's a shrewd one" or "that one sure knows what he's doing."

Furthermore, and here the fun and games are over, as Jelinek reintroduces the Angel of History with a serious warning or, as the case may be, as advise for ambitious followers of the King:

> You don't even get near the Angel, if you don't want to co-determine *the fate/destiny* of your country.[39]

> . . . dem Engel kommen Sie dann nicht mal in die Nähe, wenn Sie das *Geschick* Ihres Landes nicht mitbestimmen wollen.[40]

---

38 Jelinek, *Am Königsweg*, p. 21.

39 See pp. 48.

40 Jelinek, *Am Königsweg*, p. 21.

That is, only if you are willing to follow this leader will you get near the angel and see what you have done or will be doing—that is, contribute to the skyward growing pile of debris of history. *Geschick* translates into *fate* or *destiny*. Neither offers the same root as *schicken*. No big deal, the translator thinks at first try. There's no punning in that sentence anyway. And from the perspective of the Never-Trumper, it is a cynically true assessment of the current situation.

But—there always is still a "but"— *Geschick* as *fate* and in conjunction with schicken, *to send*, brings Heidegger into play, who fuses *Geschick* with *Geschichte* (History). And the ominous mythological resonances of the ancient Greek fate in conjunction with blind rulers out to make unsurpassable history are applicable to both Heidegger's Führer and Jelinek's King. The philosopher's etymological investigations set off the author's most mind-boggling verbal acrobatics on the topic of the use and abuse of historical legacies threatening the global future.

In the last volume of his controversial *Black Notebooks*, Heidegger derives his notion of *Geschichte*, history, from the root word, the noun *Schichte* or *Schicht*, layer, and the verb *schichten*, to layer. Against the common view of history as a sequence of cause and effect, he sees it as a *Geschicht*, a layering he compares to the layers of sediments in his beloved mountains. Seguing from *schichten* to *schicken*, to send, Heidegger transforms *Geschichte*, history, via *Geschicht* (layers) into *Geschick*, (fate / destiny) and results in the equation that

History (*Geschichte*) = Destiny/Fate (*Geschick*).[41] "Fate" comes closer to Heidegger's self-identification with ancient Greek thought, while "destiny" connects to "destination," thus still suggesting *schicken* (to send something to someone). Alas, neither term contains the root for either Heidegger's further historical ruminations or Jelinek's satirical twisting of them.

Stay with me. Jelinek does not get into a highly philosophical examination of the president. Quite the contrary: she uses Heidegger's technique to mock him and, as is her habit, also herself.

Nevertheless, she also learned a lot from Heidegger's etymological digs, his fusions of roots in archaic neologisms to express with utmost precision his philosophy in a new language that he deems necessary to express properly the depths of his thinking. But here's the important "but" again: her strategy goes much beyond mockery for its own sake. Heidegger's dense interweaving of roots provides the underpinning for his vehemently contested assertion that history is not made by the individual. Rather, one is overcome by one's destiny of being in history, that is, *Geschichtlichkeit*, historicity.

To appreciate Jelinek's subversively self-deprecating appropriation of Heidegger "speak" and its academic interpretation, I include an extensive quote from Professor Dahlstrom's more accessible explanation of the philoso-

---

41 Martin Heidegger, *Gesamtausgabe, Band 97, Anmerkungen I–V. Schwarze Hefte 1942–1948* (Frankfurt am Main: Vittorio Klostermann, 2015), pp. 47–8.

pher's notion of history and historicity as opposed to *Historie*, as it is usually studied and taught:

> History can stand for a story about, a means of recounting something in the past and therefore making it an explicit object of consciousness or knowing. All the while, the past is observed and explained from the perspective of the present. But such recounting and explanations presuppose that something happens. History can also stand for what happens itself. Thus we distinguish a historical study from a historic, i.e. history-making event. In a cognate way, Heidegger distinguishes history in the most fundamental sense of the term, i. e. *Geschichte* as happening from historical studies, i.e. Historie—and similarly historicity (*Geschichtlichkeit*) from historicality (*Historizität*). History is what happens (*geschieht*) but not, at bottom, in the sense of an occurrence in time. Rather the essence of history is historical being itself, namely, the happening of the appropriation of human beings to the presence of beings and vice versa. This happening has a beginning that is still coming to us and, in that sense, is futural.
>
> We are caught up in history and hence, it is never an object as the past is for historical studies that recount or chronicle it.[42]

---

42 Daniel O. Dahlstrom, *The Heidegger Dictionary* (London: Bloomsbury Academic, 2013), p. 96.

One of the play's key passages is a wild send-up of Heidegger's terminology that ultimately reveals Trump's perversion of tradition into something sold as new. It starts with a variation on the theme of *schicken*, sending something, that is intended to be delivered (*geliefert*), which mutates into the *Überlieferte*, a Heidegger term meaning tradition, something that has been passed on, handed down. Here the English language can be stretched beyond the available German synonyms for tradition and downgrade it to hand-me-downs, which compensates for the impossibility to match the puns Jelinek squeezes out of the root words *schicken—liefern* (send—deliver):

> So. Sind wir jetzt alle *geliefert*? Nein, nur das *Überlieferte* ist geliefert worden, das eh schon jeder kennt [. . .][43]

Literally translated, the section's opening passage reads:

> So now. Have we all been delivered? No, only that which has been passed on to us, tradition, which everyone knows already anyway.

In view of the unnamed ruler, the English language offers a temptingly ironic translation of "deliver": "to save someone from a painful or bad experience." However, this is not the case in German. Frustratingly, in the context of the previous section, the German idiom *geliefert sein* unequivocally means the opposite: "to be done in." The translator has to choose between transmitting a sense of

---

43 Elfriede Jelinek, *Schwarzwasser. Am Königsweg. Zwei Theaterstücke* (Reinbek bei Hamburg: Rowohlt Verlag, 2020), p. 60.

Jelinek's punning on "deliver", or stay within her original context. In this case, she opted for the second choice, because the following untranslatable pun *das Überlieferte* takes Jelinek into a riff on the function and abuse of tradition, which her translator is unable to deliver (!) verbatim in English. With the author's blessing, the translator is on her own. She tweaks "being done in" into "having had it," that still vaguely suggests "having got something (whatever has been sent [*geschickt*], which is the *Geschick*; i.e. the destiny/fate destined for/sent to humans). The deviation from the German original allows her to introduce a prophetic connection to the later President Trump, that is, his claim to be the savior, in answer to the question:

"So, have we all had it now? No, you just have it coming, a second coming, a tradition anyone knows already anyway [. . .] "[44] The continuation of this section is quoted in full, because it gets to the core of Trump's staging of his historic moment: from Plato's cave, peopled by human stock, capitalism's founding capital, with the market's writings on the wall, to historical stock traded in historical costume shops and presented at the White House in a charade of pompous and, as we thought, long-overcome customs in the costumes of the passed-on, the handed-down, fake hand-me-downs overcoming us as the fake New:

> So, have we all had it now? No, you just have it coming, a second coming, a tradition everyone knows already anyway. The cave we live in is quite small, everything can be seen even by a blind man, a seeing

44 Jelinek, *Am Königsweg*, p. 11.

one can look at it as writing on the wall, and those who dwell with us are asked right off what stock they come from. They say they don't know stock from Adam, but they still rule like a king, until they get freed again?, even though they just elected one, whatever. Meanwhile, the historical stock, i.e. tradition, has been traded, disguised as that which has been and will be at the same time, elected is elected and thus the past we overcame came over us like the plague that's curative, no, curable, why did it come at all?, what for?, to decide for, over us? To perform this tradition, to wit, the eternal, it has to put on a new costume that will last a bit longer, maybe all the way to heaven's gate, because here on this land it can never be eternal, here it must be harvested. It won't make it; won't it, really? A tradition cannot be altered retroactively, otherwise it would be an oracle that's known for being right in only half the cases; so the overcome arrogates to itself the move, with all its uncreative pomp, into this house only, which the ruler hasn't even built himself, who would even want to move in there?, but people almost kill each other for it, well, I say uncreative, since what came over us has long been here already, it might seem done in, but it is far from done, it is the old we already know and are now permitted to welcome as new, because it is always necessary to get a new person, even in one's own family. Thus we are told and we must accept this disgrace: being like everyone else. The King, at any rate, can't stand being like us. We are afraid of the new, it will never belong to us, nothing belongs to us anymore anyway!, what more leasing rates could there be?, how many of us can be consumed as workers without consumer protection, which the King does not grant us, what for?, he doesn't need it either. We are still waiting for what the overcome has come to arrogate to itself, just that one house mentioned before, that's not enough for us, there must be higher grounds for it, we haven't yet said for what and how all this came to be!, it should at least be coming now!, we said a lot, but not this, right? It should be saying it right here, and you would have to name it, at the top of your voice, shouted down from this platform, does it arrogate this arrogation or not, or something else that'll suddenly come over us? Well, then just about anyone could come along! We'll never come up with the rates, they got us way in over our heads, we don't even manage to give our wishes a real chance, because they already had their one and only chance. We voted, I didn't, but others did in my place, but they were not where I wanted them, they were elsewhere and made the wrong choice and such wishes must also be paid for at some point. Okay, so now we know more or less what this tradition does, do you?, I wrote this, but I don't know either. The fruit of the globe, no, of globalization are finally distributed as unfairly as possible, the disaffected grow on trees and get picked and processed into juice, that yields more than eating them raw, because for juice the mushy and rotten ones can also be used. The doings of tradition, who cares?, well, you don't know it, but I, I at least have an idea, I just can't say it, so then what does the overcome, no, that what's coming over us really do, we'd very much like to know, at least now?, and you still owe it to us, we don't like debts all that much, the banks are more likely to. Then they can really slap it on, and we'll be the ones to get hit. Move over there please, that's where you'll get it.[45]

In conclusion, a word about the most frequently asked questions:

Who Is the "You"?

In Jelinek's dramaturgy it is, of course, but not always, used in the traditional sense of addressing a real or imagined partner, or the audience. However, while the English "you" stands for second person, singular and plural, German differentiates between the intimate second person *du* and the formal third person address, *Sie*, with a capitalized *S* as well as in reference to "they," *sie*, now lowercase *s*. It becomes sometimes difficult to catch these nuances in translation. But the "you" becomes the greatest problem for the translator, when it is used in the sense of the German *man*, "one" as in "one doesn't do this," which, in most cases, sounds stilted in English and is commonly replaced with "they" or "you." It

---

45 See pp. 52–4.

gets more complicated in the English translation, haunted as it is by Heidegger. The German *man* is a foundational term in Heidegger's philosophy, referring to the anonymous persons in the crowd, the "one" merging with the crowd, indistinguishable in the masses as opposed to the figure of the leader, the Führer.

Who Are the "We" and—Who Is Speaking Anyway?

In the choral structure of the text, the "we" depends on which side is speaking and who in the audience will identify with whom. Jelinek does not designate individual characters or choral passages; these must be gleaned from the text, even though it apparently features only two speakers, Miss Piggy and later "Another woman who is bleeding from the mouth for a change." Jelinek explained this other woman to me as "the one who speaks about reality," a woman with a wounded mouth "who says what became of what Miss Piggy saw." The blind seer, "alluding of course to Tiresias, who should be a woman this time, though not a real one but a plushy, something funny. Only what she sees is not funny and what the other woman says isn't either. [. . .] As you know, my figures are not strictly separate. The two are probably the two sides of the same coin." [46] As mentioned earlier, the author also speaks through Miss Piggy, who also channels the unnamed ruler and the crowds. (Author's disclaimer: The 2016 presidential candidate Donald Trump calling a recent Miss Universe "Miss Piggy" is purely coincidental. The slur had not sunk in when Jelinek, a caring

---

46 Personal email, October 21, 2019.

collector of plushies, chose Miss Piggy, her beloved favorite, as the blind but all the more fore-sighted prophet.)

So, why not let have Miss Piggy have the last word, now in hindsight (slightly modified in the mode of her great fan): "Still a mystery to me why everybody bought Hogwash."[47]

---

47 Wikiquote entry on *The Muppets* (TV Series), adapted. Available at: http://bit.ly/3cNVsHx (last accessed on March 10, 2020).

ON THE ROYAL ROAD

THE BURGHER KING

(Vespasian? No, not that one! Cola di Rienzo? He's more likely! But, no, I'll look at the photo: Not him, either!)

(Miss Piggy, made up as the blind seer, with a cane, bleeding eyes, as tradition calls for. Altogether, I would like for the following figures from The Muppet Show. *But since this is not possible, maybe just suggestions, touches of those creatures, a psychosis perhaps, no, plush pants hanging on someone, a removable head, a nice frog, etc. Some fantasy, please.)*

Whom do I actually want to talk about, I'll have to confer with myself about that. First off, silence would suggest itself, I would prefer that, it's no work. Blindness: Also quite practical. Let me be, I see, that's what you're doing anyway, let me be, for I am ill and understand nothing, I can see, no, I can't, eyes on the balls, homerun! Poor blind me, I don't understand what I ordered here, is it a birdhouse or a new garage, at least the car port I want to let grow over with ivy, if this is what I ordered. If it is what I've got. I don't know what's coming. I don't want to talk about my mother, not ever, I couldn't care less if everything's in order with her, and I won't elaborate on it either. What fault have I committed, what debt incurred unwittingly? Well, in that regard, the

King scores much higher than I, at this time he is busy, he has to carve millions of scores into his pistol, that is, into the barrel, and did he have some barrel, out of this world! Really, nobody believes it. And none of his relatives have been bought, they do the buying themselves. When they feel like seeing the sun for once, they just go there and so they see it. No, I don't mention my mother, the father's murderess, but I helped her a little, maybe it was even more than a little. Attention, here comes the new King, quick, turn on the device!, make sure, you stupid cow, not to bring shame upon him. Watch out that he won't drive you out of the country! But that's another country, the country I am in! Oh, he'll think of something! No, he won't buy the other country, he concentrates on his homeland. I hold my hand in front of his face, he doesn't see it. He already saw nothing before. That's the proof. There he stands and no light is left for me. A pity. Still: I am speaking. No. I foresay, no, I foreswear, no, that's not it either. I just say: No one else did it. No idea, what. The King doesn't look to me as if he wanted to do anything at all. Other than default, but that is surely our fault as well. He borrowed money knowing that he will pay, no play his debts to a tee. The tee gets him to the next hole. Debts got him very far. Of course, he was a daredevil, it paid off, he made a few killings.

Run, kids, or don't run, I am no Medea, no, and no Electra either. I would not kill children. Mommy, sure, but I delegated this task to a brother I don't have. After all, the King also delegates everything, but there are things he takes into his own hand, uh-uh, not what you mean! He pays back in everyone's own coin. If someone cons him, he cons him back, but ten times as rotten, that feels good, man, what a great feeling! Oh, just do what you want. From the man's mouth you will hear that he does not want to kill but to build. Many buildings. Still more buildings. And what's this site doing here? That one has holes! Holes? That pig. Did he buy that one too, that site? He must have gotten it for a good price, there is nothing one can do with this site. Now he's calling Scotland, because he wants to buy another site there. Earlier he called Argentina, or he has been called, now he always gets called, he doesn't have to worry, now everyone wants to be in touch with him and he immediately asks if he can finally build something there too, for example something he has wanted to build for a long time. The day laughs golden, the building also laughs golden. All is gold that glitters. What, that building too? That one looks as if it tolerated neither rain nor sun or light. And it's made of pure gold. Something had to be torn down before, but that's not visible now, of course not, because people are driven to gold until they cling to it like tinsel to a Christmas tree.

What's this God talking about, what does he tell you, now you can finally see him, he foretells you a brilliant future, which you already knew, you don't need a God for that: A future, which no longer is one, it is the present. You'll get the value of your presence weighed, not in gold, there's nothing to weigh and not even that is worth the weight of what you say. Everything has weight, but who should lift it?

Only shortsightedness and the constant need to beef could assume that this is just a specific, if random worldview of someone sufficiently aggressive, who'd enforce his view hell-bent. He is about to start, just pulled the club out of the wrapping. Help, my self-assurance is also coming to life now! And you will also get used to the feeling of feeling good. Just to make sure, we put a populist stamp on it and off it goes. Those coins are being issued now, there, look!, the self-assured folks get the same thing on both sides, this coin is valid only for the bringer, but he can't buy anything with it. He's been bought himself, and even paid for it himself! A rare feat!—The generosity alone in the name of the father and his two sons, who grew like trees to heaven and no one noticed, costs!—There is a goal to accomplish, after all! Everybody has a father whether he knows him or not, but this father can be procured provided your profits fit the bill. It all goes hand in hand, both of which are held out, one pulling this way, the other that way, so that the money can rain into them and bring blessings. These hands are always open. Their owners are not. They are just taking.

No, no, say it again, please, then we'll better understand what's not supposed to be understood. Beefers be gone! Whine-os, stop pissing. Keep it inside your pants, oh, right, there's no more room. The bottom, that's what you are yourselves. What is it that's been pulled off here because so many pulled on it? Is this an episode, no, a hit, no, the expression of a serial hitter, so then expression or obsession?, what is it now?, of the existential will, no, the existential unwillingness of the subjectivity of the subject, the subjects, all of them without a consciousness, and if you are unconscious, anyone can cut you crosswise, drill into you, pierce you, scratch you all over, you won't notice. Something hits, but it misses, unfortunately, still, it keeps hitting, undaunted, it hits on every feeling, because that's all it is, they can't do more than feel, those who cherished and chose you. So now that world view will turn for those who don't know the world, because they never viewed the world turning in a soap, that world view turns into, well, what does it turn into, spit it out!, it turns, let's take a look, no idea what that's supposed to be, I, at any rate, have something else, a different world view, now the King will say what has often been said: Old age is a massacre, can't even look at you, awful!, well, then I'll just hide behind my world view, which I often showed off with. A world for show, as it turns out now, is becoming the definitive, sole world view we've got, after all, we don't have another world to view and now will you finally show yourself!, you are quite a looker, why are you hiding? Oh Lord, now we finally get it—why you've been hiding from us for so long! It is because of the hairdo! You need a different coiffeur! You are a nightmare! And better too, your mouth would stay shut. Rather, let's turn to those who don't have to hide themselves, who haven't been touched yet by the darkness of death, who are not tarnished, who can last a bit longer.

Who are those turning up all of a sudden! They are taking off, they take up arms, they take themselves out, no, not that, they cover our silence and scream. They scream out everything they know, luckily it doesn't last long. Only until the white paint dries with which they whitewashed themselves, in case their original color was different. Let's hope it covers as well as indicated on the bucket. So. Here they are. Not a minute too late! Finally! They are showing themselves and their world view, which someone like you doesn't have, it's under the whitewash. Should we add another layer, at least give it a thought?

The view is looking for someone who needs one. Most people have got one already. They paid enough for it, now it is finally worth something. What kind of forces are those beginning to be effective? You don't say, someone's hanging on a tree? This can't be collective violence, no, no, and there, entire packs are crossing the border, masses of them, weapons to the masses!, but quite a few people are still needed to balance this out. There are more weapons than people. Or maybe not. I don't know. When collective forces are at work, they are already consolidated and get cracking, let's roll! Violent unanimity, is that what caused this? Apparently. But such unanimosity vanishes completely behind the myths and the lies that bubble out of the TV, the man speaks, he is his own religion, now you can throw away the one you've got. God is here. Don't underestimate him! You'll still need him, so then he better be powerful. Or you'll be lost. Consider all the capital, no, not that one—you couldn't even imagine that one, let alone consider it; rather, consider the pent-up hate-potential, the pent-up distrust, and if people are drawing from it, a new being gets drafted, the

King takes shape who is prepared any time for the violence of his neighbors and will therefore return the neighbors to the neighbors. Thanks.

Anything the neighbor does just proves to us that the neighbor has aggressive tendencies. We deport him. Or we are as aggressive to him, or more so, or more frequently. Since this is what he is planning against us, it is only just. The violence for which we prepare ourselves by turning it against those violent ones before they turn against us, violence has such power, it won't vanish on its own. It can't do it. It is here to stay.

Life goes on, folks go away, life is inexplicable. It is inexplicable to me how life keeps moving, why it won't keep still, always wanting to catch a view of something. The view expands, everything is going too fast to gain such a view or another—the latter, however, doesn't count, that lottery we lost already. Deny people force and they'll be the first to turn against you to get it back again. Force is their favorite hobby and it's also a nice profession. They cast their vote, but don't know who they voted for, even though they did it themselves. They voted for someone with a certain view in the hope he would let them keep the violence, the only thing they have and exercise and execute. They take their liberty, they take up their arms, they attack everybody and afterwards it all gets covered with silence like a pile of dog shit with leaves. And then the next one steps into it. Things are not as bad as they look or—as the saying goes elsewhere, nothing's eaten as hot as it gets cooked. Just ask the cook. Life's inexplicability explains why we can't view things without getting them explained to us. How come? Earlier, on the net, things looked so good and now it's all gone, even the preview of a view—it's even the one we had hoped for, the King has exactly the same!—from whose high horse we can always only gain something nobody else wants. Who's got it, where is it, the view, someone's got to have it, pray who?, the world simply must be viewed in order for one to get a view, you don't have one, where on earth could you get it if you always stay at home and are even afraid of red traffic lights, while it was at a green one where you thought yourself safe, you were almost run over. This could never happen to us, we always count on an attack in order to preempt it, we adapt to the King and now we have adopted his view, it was ours to a tee, just that he's got more of them, more views, so he has enough to change. Like underwear. He tells us that already earlier we thought like him who never thinks. Everything we already had before returns to us as a threat: more show of force. The King is in charge of it and applies it and he is not for sharing it. He just decided this once and for all, thus validating you to the very end. And all others expire. Have expired. For violence is not something external, in case you have observed it with children, the way they share shovel and sand bucket, voluntarily, and yet, the very next moment the bucket including its contents fly in the playmate's face. Violence is not superficial, even though we would like to think it is, it fuses, it has long fused, it goes in very deeply and then down, wherefrom very dark forces emerge and fuse with your cancer, with your losses of people and stocks, the earthquake in Italy or wherever, it meets your own violence, which is also ready to break out and mow down everything any time, even though the grass you don't want to have, you don't want your neighbor to have either, this innocent, immaculate grass, which does nothing but grow—yes, the dandelion in it unfortunately does too—has nothing done to you, except being there and having also brought you the dandelion and you didn't like that. Go get the reaper, get the mower that makes such a racket; it runs on gas and no one inspects the exhaust, what's coming out of there, after all, they do that with cars, inspect and adapt the motor to the inspection, why, the inspection can't adapt to the motor, can it now?, see, you can already see with me how violence meets violence in me; it is always there, waiting. Waiting to be let out. The neighbor gets my leaves blowing around his head, great, serves him right, he deserves it for his stupid grass. I don't know how the grass is supposed to be stupid, that's far beyond my brain, stupid me!, for getting at the rot, no root of this, brains no longer strive for something, hands don't reach out; we lost, my brain understands how grass is the way it grows, but that grass including weeds clearly reaches further, it reaches me, it hands me the weapon which I immediately aim at the disgusting weed. It's gotta go. Everything's gotta get out. And shoot! So start up the mower, right, yes, got myself another blood blister on the heel of my hand, it's where the hand ends and the fingers want to start working but can't do it, there's nothing there for them to do. I don't even feel that kind of thing. I am totally on foreign territory with this, well, just as I had in mind. Where's the violence? Go, get the ball! Grrrrrr! There it is. Good. We can really use it. It's all we've got.

In case you are looking for your world view, we have it, you can get it or a similar one, whatever we have right now, any time. But it's painful to look at the world!, horrible!, take our specs from our brand optician, not from the other one, who also carries brands, but they have expired, they have lost their appeal but that's all there is for poorer folks if they also want to see something they don't understand. Look through this certified glass, the fit doesn't matter, you can throw one any time, it's the glass that'll cut it for you, straight to the bone, then you'll be able to see better; so, one more time, but I don't remember the first time, which already happened several times and pushed itself to the front as if it were new again or like new: World-viewability, no, you've got that already, but now it shall be the world-feudability that just turned world-view, you can shove that up yours and thus show yourself to the world, so that you can be moved forward and clearly seen in front of the viewing platform. That's a really good view. Better than what we'll get to see. If we'll get anything? No. Today the world won't show itself to you. Come back tomorrow.

The path-breaker shows himself but he doesn't know what he broke, why and how he should be ahead of all the others, he doesn't understand it, he was no frontrunner, he just likes breaking things, but now he's got them and doesn't know what to do with them. He certainly fought, together with his good-looking wife, for lookers, and he got them, he can get them all and stick his fingers into them, he can have his fingers in everything and play them as they lay, he gets everything, he gets them all. He shows himself, go ahead, look at him, don't shy away from this sight, you'll get to see worse ones!, as the path-breaker of a certain political and nativist style, nonsense, not nativist, he does not have to emphasize the nativist aspect, there is only one nation in the world, one *Volk*, that goes without saying, we are not in Germany now!, been there, done that, it's over. So, the nativist stuff is a non-issue, he can also say I or we, maybe he also says: The *Volk*, but that's us, pardon me, we are of course a different *Volk*, not the one we were, but one and at one with each other we are not either, as little as the *Volk*, the *Reich* and the new Führer. That he is new already shows he is not dangerous, the dangerous ones had their turn already, so many had to take their clue from us in order to take us to court, but that's over, nothing to be done about that. Okay, so the path-breaker has finally come, he has arrived, the urns have decided for him, when they were emptied there were no ashes in them, strange, he fought his way to the front and right through it, his mouth opened and closed again, it happens to all of us, and now hardly anyone can see him anymore, he has gotten way out of sight, wind and fog are his allies. One can't see anything, we are blown away by the new wind like his *speak*, well maybe everything gets blown off before he can blow it all up and he'll be really out of sight. But there are other possible reasons for not seeing him—because folks were looking for him in the wrong place. So, now, folks, choose your path-breaker, the path doesn't count anyway, only the breakthrough and he made it and not that woman, who kept hitting the roof but could not break through the ceiling. So, people, pick your path-breaker now, it's not the path that counts, only the breakthrough. And he contests it. He contests everything, now is the right time to contest everything, yes, even the university for the sale of buildings, which however always only cheated and sold people, that will be settled now, but you better believe him, he will pay you back for this too. Eventually your turn will be first, no doubt, that is, if you nicely keep in line, if you deftly walk the line, however far it goes. But here is your path-breaker. I personally gave him lip, since then he is the only one talking, now you've just got to listen to him, then you can chase after him for all I care, end of story, if you love me, follow me, but all the others too. Well, that is not what he wanted. Did you vote already? We did, thank you very much. Tomorrow will be someone else's turn, though it'll take a while until tomorrow and then someone else will sniff the sun coming out tomorrow and step up to us, isn't that nice of him.

And at bottom, even the opponents and the backward-looking will somehow move on, but they don't know whereto; no, they don't have to turn around, those are the kind that have headlights on their back rather than in front so that no one would kill them from behind while they are tilling their field, which already belongs to the bank, yes, the house too, that's been taken already by those forging ahead, who just wanted to have it all and took it away from them, because they couldn't get it anywhere else, they did not get it back to how it was before and where they want to go back to pigheadedly, they do still have their car, it is piled up high with belongings for which they have no home, it is the bank that owns it now. The interests were higher than the house, no, than the value of the house. If you pack anymore on the roof of your automobile, there'll be an auto-da-fé. Then everything will go up in flames because the vehicle can't breathe anymore. No idea, where it'll get the oxygen. For what do you need a pathbreaker when all you are is broke and dying to get back, to where the wooden fence with the lopsided For Sale sign blocks your view, you wouldn't really want to buy back your own house, would you? No more house, no more shelter, no truth, no property. Tell me, are you testing me now? I can explain why we all belong to the banks, which had to be saved before, because if they hadn't been saved we would have been safe. Let's move on, we have to anyway, it's just a bit difficult with that big trailer. Our car is a bit too weak to pull it, even though the old time is pulling away with us. We no longer see the new one. Others don't yet see it. We no longer do.

Go ahead, walk right through the masses, they won't split for you and they won't split anything with you. You cannot see your leader at this time because you are storming ahead so blindly, because you think there is something to get for nothing, you don't know what, you only know that something is given, an election gift, which is not a gift you'd have selected, but who is checking when something is for free. He does his thing with gifts to make you think you can chase after him, whereas he is already after you by now. When he thrusts himself forward, there will be cohesion, no, such coherence existed before, now there is a furious collision, a crash between those who push back, because their leader is behind them and those who press forward because they haven't yet caught on that he is now pushing from behind, if only they'd know whereto, tsk, tsk, now you make him a scapegoat, just because you don't know where he is, or could he have vanished into thin air? You've gotta be kidding! Where the hell did he go? Fuck him! We'll fuck him over like we got fucked, which did not take a village, well, so we didn't make it in the city, we hate the city, because it didn't let us in, it didn't even let us near it. Now we exercise violence, it is the essence of violence that it demands surrender, utter surrender, yes, and even exercise, or we could not exercise it. We still look at violence as something external, while it is inside us, it is already inside us, we surrendered to it and then it wasn't even our lover. We'd have never wanted a horrible type like that, did you see his face, his hair? That's not what we wanted, we never wanted that, but we got him and now he is inside us, we sacrifice for him, we sacrifice ourselves to him, but this sacrifice does not appease him. He wants to continue to live in his sky-fucking-scraper with all that gold, I don't think it's real because there is so much of it. And from there he will call us to order.

Go ahead, you starter of sensational pleasures, step on the gas!, isn't that also exactly where you wanted to go? Back? Backwards? So why are you pushing like that? I don't get it, but what do I know. Now someone is carried past. No idea.

It must be the opponent, the backwards striver per se in search of his braces, or else he will drop, so those are carried by a person's world-viewability, isn't that the truth, no, not true, we had that once already—that something wasn't the truth but we still insisted on it, so then man carries his world-viewability on his back, no matter if it's viewable or not, the world's always around, he better view the world calmly before its owner arrives and threatens us with a weapon, but we have our own weapon, because everybody has one, to each his own. Everyone has his own facts and everyone else also has his facts, but different ones. Of course they are not the same, but both are true. Thus everybody has a weapon against everybody. A no-brainer. We were told he'd never be elected and we believed it! He can vote alright, but he will never be chosen, you guaranteed this to us, and now the warranty has supposedly expired already?, it only expires in two years when the device falls apart, that's already scheduled, that way you can look on how the mendacious notions that something would last forever are shattered by their own predetermined breaking point. And you can also recognize how much strength they had, now that it's too late and you have to dispose of the device which broke not by your violence, but all on its own. And that poses even more problems for you. It's all outdated now, it hasn't been updated, or it would be like new again. I think I've got something in my eye.

They calculated their winner, who are they anyway? And who is the winner? The man of aggression, which he himself looks at indifferently, he applies it but it is not applied to him, he can be sure of that. They authorized him as their winner and there he is, the winner and his entire family, they are also coming on board, even if they aren't coming now and then, although the TV is always there, it's already been there for a while, it must focus on him after all, calibrate the sharpness, that's done very quickly today. The King is already sharp enough. And the mindlessness of his supporters' calculations, those who elected him, comes clearly to light on this freshly printed receipt streaming out of the cash register and it is wrong, this receipt, too little has been noted and netted, because one fan in tow is not enough, towing a trailer can be done by any car that's strong enough to carry a tennis ball on the tow bar, I can't see the purpose of it, aha!, I still can't see it, but its function is to protect the part that's sticking out under the bumper to protect the other cars from itself, we often think we protect ourselves while we actually protect others, embarrassing!, often it can't do it, carry the tennis ball, towing the trailer, I already said it, when the driver is too weak for it, then the trailer tows the towing vehicle, doesn't it?, and not the other way around, one can lose one fan in tow, one just has to give voice to the fan base, this has been done herewith, I don't have more to say about that, yes, and this impotence, no, sorry, I mean of course, this—as I already said before—mindlessness, this uncontrolled mindlessness we observe now has been disguised as a historic costume like those CliniClowns with their red clown noses—you can't really see what's behind it, but you have an inkling, if you know the respective person, the light gets diffuse, everyone sees something else in the background, through the fog, something that looks as if it had always been there, as if the power that's behind it were eternal the way it is, as if all of this had already existed forever. As if people had always already known the truth of someone else and condemned it, never recognizing it as their own. While the truth is only there to be recognized, no matter in what disguise and were it only a small, unimportant site, where towers fell.

That was a good thought, albeit not mine; how come the customized costume has again not be delivered by—?, we paid for it three weeks ago, by credit card, though our credit has long been exhausted and we could not buy anything for it and had to get ourselves delivered, drone by drone to drone, a victory of convenience? Mindlessness, however, is senseless, we lost our mind for no reason at all, and if we came to our senses, it did not help, or it was too late then, rethinking never helps, it's like picking up chewed gum and chewing it again, with all the dirt that sticks to it. The past can no longer be delivered, this is it, it didn't run out, it's here already, after all, though different from what it's ever been. It has become unrecognizable. It lost its form completely. What does the King say? We should get him out, hide him, kill him, throw him in the ocean, whatever. He isn't serious, don't worry. We should just get used to it, that this is what he has in mind with others. The King uses violence against himself just to get us used to this violence being used against us later. And no sacrifice will reconcile us again. And the proposition, no, the presentation that everyone can be man and woman at once, if he just wants it, just as he wants it, nothing is fixed, only eternity threatens us all the same, this presentation will be given in the lecture hall today, though, unfortunately, we won't hear it, even though all the visuals are in place. The lecture will be cancelled and other than that, no one says anything.

The only difference between the King and his opponents— and here the one cannot be the other—I vouch for this with my name, that is, for healthy children's food: Hip-hip-hur- ray—consists in that, chronologically, the King appears first and, as of this moment will always come first before all oth- ers. Thus we decreed and thus we inaugurate our new creed. That's all there is to it. Do you want to hear the latest oracle? So you don't. You still have to chew on yesterday's, which already today turned out not to be true. I thought so. No need for it anyway, watch out! Why should we know some- thing, where knowledge is useless and worthless and sense- less and anyway? Oh, had we never come! But here we are and fill the seats and yell and sacrifice and violate, because everyone should be active in some way. That's good for one's body, unfortunately not for those of others. Who will lead us? We know that other leader and don't want him. The one we want we don't get. The thinker wanted to lead the leader but lost him halfway, because he overlooked a signal all other peoples had heard except him, lost him in a place where he had no place, poor thinker. It wouldn't have worked anyway, one mind stopped working on his own, he was insulted that he could not be in the driver's seat although he just got his license, but not for the truck and now he is a truckload for the leader, oh dear, he didn't want that!, no, instead he wanted to be more—no, he is no more, I mean *not* more— he is the one who is always led on by the leader, that is, the other way around. The thinking collapses without the thinker having noticed. And if he needed it he hasn't got it, it doesn't work properly, the wrong date had been entered in the warranty and the thinker is already kaput before we could hear him talk. The blind seer, by contrast, can be led, he actually needs it, without a leader the seer would not manage seeing nothing, of course he doesn't see a thing. That is his nature, seeing nothing, as all of us see nothing, so then who should lead him until he's got rid of his infamies? I can see it already, I don't see it, of course, but I see it in an internalized way, with eyes that shine inwards: This man possesses the truth, which is a mystery, which is no mystery, we have been told long ago and unfortunately passed it on wrong, in any case not as we've heard and not understood it either. We don't yet have a license, we only have our drives and protective padding for our bed, so that nothing leaks and we stay at home at night and can attack our loved ones, like Medea. But now I insert myself again, I shouldn't do that. And children were not delivered to me, amazon claims they got lost in transit. Fine with me. Oh, but I do have my license, on paper, I've got the tool, the towel for cleaning the hallway, the bathroom and the kitchen table, all with one and the same! I completely forgot about it. We've always known that we know it, whatever it may be, and has it been useful and did we need the blind seer for that? No.

Well, I know one thing: This man has not killed any relatives. We know this for sure, all of them are still around and standing in front of cameras lined up like dogs in dog training are not, they'd first have to be yelled at. And this I can see in the seer, no, not that one, but your foxy, tell-all televisionary, I can see this in the King from far away: It is absolutely impossible for him to have married his mother, his mother would not be worth a marriage to him, she would be far too old and ugly, he would never touch her, all skin and bones, no, bones without skin, what does that woman there claim?, that he touched her?, he'd never have done it, anyone can see that she is not his cup of tea, moreover, she is dead and furthermore, related to him. He doesn't need that. He gets the best service anywhere. Only the younger and more beautiful are getting married, they are instantly recognizable anywhere, we don't need a seer for that and we don't pay him either for telling us what he found out, what all of us have known all along and can see any time on Face the Nation, no, Facebook. You will get to know the truth that goes with it, you will hear it, maybe not from me, well, definitely not from me, because I don't know it, I knew it once, when it was still very little, but now we haven't seen each other in a long time. You will hear it for sure, you will hear truth collapse, because no one has supported but always only defamed it. You won't be able to see it anymore, because you will be blind, and not even your blindness will be your own doing, it will have been inflicted upon you. Say what?, you want to have the same blindness as the seer, just in another color? We don't have it. The King bought up all the blindness, because he saw its advantages. One can believe a blind man anything he says, he is incapable of lying, because he never gets to know the truth. Does all this come from his brain or is it another's invention?

The blind one believes that truth possesses power and strength, that's how he imagines it, because he is the only one who tells it as it is. And all of us get plunged into misery anyway. Okay, so the King slays the seer, so that he, the King can become blind himself, so he can finally be the only blind person. Even blindness he does not grant anyone else. No one gets to have a voice, he strikes up his own song and tweets it out, more than a hundred times the hour, he's got the final word alright. For when the King pronounces it, it doesn't matter what he sees or says. It's right in any case. When the King is blind, what is it you want to see, when even the King can't see a thing. There's nothing to see. He has seen it all, he has taken a look at it all and then decided. So why turn blind at all? It doesn't pay off, small change is all fate ever pays, but when you check your statements, no, not yours, the bank's, of course,—who cares about yours!,—after you moved out of your house, you are still receiving your bank statements, at whatever address, that's when you notice: Fate does not take cash, it wants wireless payment, so then it's just for show? Yes, but it has nothing to show for it. So, where did all the coins go which at least looked like and weighed a lot. Gone to bits. What?, everyone blind? The King blind and his subjects too, all of them? The seer also blind? Who then still sees anything in this nation which rules so many, which rules so many countries, any way he likes it, wherefore they do not like him, but he doesn't care, some get deported, others deposited in a place where he needs them, the next ones he doesn't let in at all, others he sets up so that he will not be the one to blame; we are told and shown who is who, but if you can't see them, couldn't they also be someone else? How's a blind one to know? Like me? Well, I think, a blind seer, a woman, is indeed a remarkable change from seeing to knowing without ever having seen. That is my fate. Whatever, they all must get out, then it's our turn, patiently we act stupid, the King wants it that way, but he wants to be unforeseeable, how does he put it, better than I as usual?, no one will touch us, move us?, reach us?, I want to join, because I am so unforeseeable and already able to see just with the spoon, I don't yet dare to try with the knife, that's already blinded quite different folks than me, I rather am the blinding one. Why? Because—is what he says. But all of us will say Merry Christmas and a Happy New Year! There will no longer be anyone not believing in the ruler's birth, which actually started the calamity. But he doesn't remember it. He can't remember his birth, which was followed by terrible events. Our life is based on this: that we won't be able to remember. The environment's protection will disappear, the unborn's will come. The wall along the gigantic border, no, both are gigantic, wall and border, made of Heidelberg cement, the world's best, because it craves so much for *Bildung*, no, binding, this wall will rise, water and gravel added, yes, lime too, how else could we cover so many corpses?, done, the wall, bigger than we could ever imagine, it will be born so that the others can no longer be born, at least not here with us. We are an American. We are one American. But now no longer. This path won't be easy and it will be blocked to boot. We will fuck it up for them, or force it down their throat, in the Rio Grande. We'll make them swallow it, and the money for it which we won't spend, because the neighbor will have to spring for it, we will give to our veterans who fought so hard for us and still lost, those idiots, at any rate, they'll get the money, whether they earned it or not, they didn't earn it, because they were wounded so badly. They didn't ask what their country could do for them, they did it for their country. They let themselves get wounded, those fools, how can one wage war with such people. The King will show them how it works and how things work, he will file complaints against them all, but really all. But if another woman complains, then we will too, of course, though we won't know why. We won't believe what they assured us and we will put an end to it. We will also put an end to what has been ensured by our founding fathers; we'll put an end to everything and start with something new, no matter what it is and no matter how long it will take for the dust to settle over these events which we'll still have to decide, otherwise the events would not know where they should occur.

Okay, cut to the positive. The children, however, might be included in the insurance, the King assures us on a whim and with his mighty wham. And why? Because I say so, but I am not I, I don't have a son, no son will die at the hand of the

King, the King will not be the son who dies, I don't know, you have the choice of three paths, pick one, then give birth in peace and quiet, no in disquiet give birth to the savior, then tie his legs together and throw him, watch, that's how it's done, you take the legs, like a purse, at the handle, right, then take him up a nearly impassable mountain, oh my God, there is none?, then go look for one!, what's so difficult about that! Beating the defenseless whose hands are tied, yes, and now the legs as well, what's the problem? What are you saying? You won't be the murderer of your children, there are too many and you'll still need some to rule, as one can always rule over one's own children, you can always shut up your own kids but what do you do with the rest, all the other dumb shits? I'd say, better no mouth than no eyes, at least as far as I am concerned. Yes, also the daughter, she too gets directed and abreacted, she especially, we don't have to pro- cure her, we know where to get her, we already have her, there she is! You reach into her and right away she barks at you. She yells at you. She doesn't put up with anything. So let her be! You have nothing to fear from her or has it been the other way around, did she have something to fear from you? The father's child, in this case a daughter, so every- thing's wrong anyway with what's been said by the blind singer, no, seer. So then, the father says to the seer: It's your fault. And the seer replies: No, yours, that's called a tie, the best we are able to achieve in soccer, so there she stands, the daughter and hears the verdict and jangles her bangles, no big bang here, when will I finally stop this nonsense with words?, they stand there at the lectern but refuse to say

anything, come on!, I also have to have a little fun writing,
surely you can understand this, I am not using a buzz-saw,
which can cause unspeakable misery, I don't have boards,
what?, those?, those boards are crooked, too crooked even
for a coffin no matter how thick they are, they are unusable,
there is blood all over them, but we were talking about the
daughter, no, she won't let us, and even though she is blessed
among women, a daughter has absolutely no freedom of
action. Okay, freedom as much as she is given, but she does
not have any freedom of action. Sure, she can have action
or play-act, she can also be free, I'd rather she won't and
rather keep distributing her bracelets, which should not stay
with her, but she cannot take action. Can't do it. That girl
would never kill the father, doesn't have what it takes.
Fathers have every reason to suspect the worst of their sons,
but not of those, not from the daughter either, the worst is
not expected from them, others will have to do that. The
King is not naked, he is blind. Who would have thought that
a blind man, a blind blinder, who has inflicted everything
upon himself, even the blinding and except for his hair and
the banks, which he often cut, better than his own hair, that
such a one would even have opponents? What does he do to
not have opponents? A king needs opponents, he grows on
them. At first everybody seemed to be his opponent, that
was our fault, our delusion to think we were all of us.
Wherever all are, there always are still more of those. And
we are not all of us and it is not all over with us.

Every one of us rejects him, the King already knows that, but he doesn't believe it and I only know those who reject him, everyone around us, that is those I know think he is able to join forces with the forces let loose now or maybe not or are enforced directly by him, well, who else? All good, finally a revolution is in the making, we've needed one for a long time, or, as of this moment you would sleep another fifty years!, Revolution?, too soon to tell. We are still hearing the King's promises and won't let him keep them. We will tear them, still hot, from his hands. He will watch over the women, he says, because he respects them, women for him!, he grabs for what he just heard: Woman! My spirit confused, shaken my heart, what am I—a divorced man—to do? There are so many women, okay, now you are the only one, but the others are also always at hand, so that one can play pretty melodies on them, on their fingerboard. We never take a vacation when we are King and we don't take any money for it and we live somewhere very different, so we won't be found. There is the throne but that's not where we're jumping, we only spring disaster there. And that's the best of all, we don't take any money. We already have the money for it. We already have the kind of money it takes. And if the bank has it, it must give it. Then again it has to dispense with a lot, that's how it is with banks, down today, up tomorrow so that we must look up to them.

We'll get that woman behind bars, our opponent, and if it's the last thing we are going to do, well, maybe not the last thing, but for her it will be the last she will see of us: A closed door with guards in front of it, so she won't get out. But then again, no one asks for her either. Okay, let's keep her inside, that's where she belongs. Make-up no longer belongs on her face, the hairdresser lost his rights and was sent to the desert where he can coif cactuses. Let's forget her, she can no longer weaken our legitimacy, her goose is cooked. It was decided by much, but not too much *Volk*, many thanks that you spoke out for the King so decidedly, so that he won't have to say much more. The King cannot become good without losing his malicious sides, which one of them will he turn to us now? To the Syrians?, who's that now?, I said Syria not Syriza, that man simply can't keep them apart, will he now turn to the troublemakers, whom we first don't let in and then not out again, like that Russian, we don't want him and still, he is here, where?, well that one we do want, other Russians maybe not. So then, do we really want him, do we want all of them? No idea. I must have misunderstood something, I think, so then the carps, no, not them, the carpers, the troublemakers, who are still outside must not get in, and those in must get out, straight into the ocean for all I care, where they fall in and get cleaned out, but who cleans up the ocean after them, those whimpering non-swimmers who foul up everything?, that's just like them. But the fish are happy at least. Well, something like that, it doesn't have to be exactly that way. Now I will continue the seer's sayings, indeterminate like a plant am I before they stick me with an instrument I don't know how to play. Or maybe I should do something completely different, what do you think?, the seer's sayings have long been fixed, nowadays their foils get projected onto the wall, but I don't know how to do this, so why then should I write them down?, as I don't even know how to get them to you. Oh, I see, there they are, not where you are looking, not on the floor, that's just worn down by your life which tells you that you should have stepped down long ago, no, the wall, you've got to look at the wall!, something gets thrown at it, there they are, the sayings, there they are already, their the fleeting electrons took flight to, all other surfaces were decorated with pictures. Those stupid sayings, they don't have to first be nailed, they stand, even walk all on their own and now they stick, one way or other, exactly how we want it and what we want from them. We don't need seers, we have a net anyone gets caught in who gets into it blindly. The net shows up his boundaries, which lie in his own out-of-bounds-ness. It's been everywhere already, wherever you were looking, whatever your relatives are doing, whom you can call anytime. Better not. Help yourself! Dig in! You simply cannot miss this, but you mustn't picture it like spokes of a wheel that smash your hand if you reach into them. It's rather like a light, the same or primordial or equiprimordial particles are working hard right now turning the light on and off again, just as you like it. The fridge takes care of the cat food on its own, this is the *caring concern*, because it also carries it out according to the thinker (who sums it up as *solicitude*). Very practical. If you know what I mean. So let's hide this egg for now. Happy Easter and off to the Bunny Club. Well, then, how does the light help the blind? It's rather like plucking the air, no resistance, but everything is there, everything is ready, the devices

work on their own, why order a seer, or being a seer one-
self?, especially since everybody is blind anyway, among the
blind no blind man can be king, he only thinks he can, the
blind King, who wants to turn off the net altogether anyway,
or parts of it, yes, better just parts of it; the blind are all the
same, they think they are the top of the crop at least until
the topping out ceremony as they call the Last Judgment,
then they can all go through the roof and pat each other's
shoulders, if they find them, for having gotten through it.
Now something gets said, the opposite right after, all in a
seamless succession, everything that gets said is true and
everything is wrong, for what would we still need seers?
We don't need them. We even outfoxed television. We can
spread our own far-flung visions all by ourselves or land in
someone else's net, we already know how to upload the far
away, where we'll finally be comfortable. They tell us, and
it's always been that way, they tell us: You are guilty, but he
is guiltier. You owe, but he must own up.

The blind is talking to the blind, the net has been set up for
orientation so that no one falls over the cliff. If one turns off
half of it, a catastrophe can be the result if people have still
been in it, for example a few hundred Polish construction
workers without helmets, with helmets it would have been
too expensive, they already had sledgehammers, so they
could not reject the suggestion to do it without, it's cheaper
that way, nonsense, the other way around, more expensive,
well, but everything has been turned upside down already,
nothing fell out; okay, so a hole has been created, something
is missing, but it certainly will be filled soon; he eliminated

it immediately, lest he be eliminated, but beyond that it's spreading, the disorder is spreading, since much slips through a net that must be swept under it. Maybe the King doesn't yet know that he can't just eliminate the one—his half—so easily, no, since you are asking: He is either a zero or the first, both together don't work together: In the beyond you don't have this net, nothing holds you there, at best you'll be held up and can't go further, someone's always waiting at the gate, who might be on duty today, will he be tough?, oh dear, you'll be drifting in like those Syrtaki or whatever their name is; slowly the army of those blessed with money, those with privilege and privy, no, they are shitting all over you in public, well, they are pushing ahead, the others are facing the eye of the needle. Those, however, are too blind to thread their way through, the damned that is, no, the others are in heaven, they are shoving a bit now, because some stickler sits at the gate pressing for taxes and insisting on the release of something, otherwise the King won't get to be one, well, okay, so he will reveal himself, he reveals he earned so little it's not worth mentioning—that year even I earned more!, the gatekeeper says that a lawsuit can only be harmful, and money talks, the Syros, is this where we were?, no, luckily we aren't, we are not in heaven either as you may have assumed and as I originally insisted, no, District Court, the gyros, no, the Syrtians, those are *the* specialists in fleeing, they know already from the outset where they'll have to line up for their turn to come faster, they downloaded an app for it. They're coming from every-where, they are also getting everywhere, where they get photographed and fingerprinted. Or like that fireman who just came to my mind—though nothing should come to my mind anymore or this whole thing will get too long—okay, so, yes—the fireman and the net—this fireman, with his completely disfigured, scarred face gets removed from the other site again and again. Condemning him for his looks is an outrage, a scandal, even though the man still has his complete field of vision, for he is not blind as the King, he only looks terrifying, like without ears and other things everyone would need; yes, that's what he looks like without having ever been a race driver, so then, like that firefighter who keeps getting removed from the book of faces and thus of facts, though it's not his fault he got mangled so badly. But— we are sorry, he just doesn't have a face, I don't know how to put it differently—at least not one he should be showing, he lost it. Just as he gets constantly removed from the net, even though he gets put there precisely because he has no face, the sight of him is not acceptable for a seeing person, for a seer maybe, he can't see him anyway. Woe to you, ridiculing me for my affliction, which everyone will soon ridicule you for! This is so mean, says the King, who is still pretty complete, except for his eyes and his bank accounts, those are his problem. He sees nothing, but doesn't have to look at anything either. The King's body is complete, well almost, it's just that not everything functions. I don't have to say more, but will keep saying it about a hundred times.

So then, use the support you are getting here from the net, at least in your half, grab as much as you can as long as you can and your face has not yet been destroyed by world fires and your body by firewater! Then even the blind know where they have to go and what they should see but can't. Now all of us will be led to the abyss and may look into it, except, that is, those eyeless, visionless blind, who of course need to follow someone, they just don't know whom and where, but we should not fall into that bottomless hole either, where at some point a new super high-rise is to be placed, no, no, it's already there to wipe out the shame of the first one. Anyway, something was erected in that hole, the basement levels will be cooked in the books. There's no turning back now and no stopping. He says: I am the truth and the life. Now I will also reveal the truth, of course not the one about myself, but about all the others; I am the truth and the life, he that follows me is okay; he who doesn't isn't. That one is fired and can start fires himself or let himself be consumed by fires, as he likes it. The King just has to aerate the passed over, those preterites (pace Pynchon) for him that's a cinch, he doesn't even have to create a lot of hot air, it'll heat up later. Only I tell the truth, I alone, I have been legitimized, here is my King's ID which has been forged for a long time, but now no longer, now it's the real thing, now it became the truth, elect is elect. I don't permit the coronation of another king, but somehow I don't want to be one either. I don't need it. Omygod, now a landslide just moved half my golf course into the Pacific. Hold it, no, it was only the eighteenth hole, that's supposed to be half a billion? Okay, fine with me, that's what we tell the amazed public, we won't tell the IRS. You'd have to add on half the state to make this course as expensive as I say. If it won't slide down as well, then the price is right. I don't allow someone else having more votes than I, because I am always right, nothing is right, except I and people should be allowed to be happy about it. Okay, here it is written and there too, I was chosen, not the others, especially not that woman, and here I am. I must have my ID ready and show it, even though everyone knows me, so that I won't get expelled from this country, which I have in mind, but not for me.

Because that's coming next, people with their poor religious thinking and even poorer knowledge will simply be thrown out. Yes, you are right, I judge life from such a high horse, someone should throw me down, it might still happen, because much too often I speak my mind, and sometimes I am out of my mind, which I don't show and sometimes don't know, that's what I always say when I am asked about the net worth of my wealth, did I stick to the truth then?, I stuck to something, but don't remember what it was. I try to hold on to the truth if nothing else works, but how can you hold on to something that keeps swaying? A fortune sways, it rises and falls with the markets, the climate, the dominant feelings with one's own feelings, with the weather report, how can you hold on to something you can't find, because you don't even know it, how can you know the truth if you've never seen it? How would you recognize it? Am I supposed to look for it? I certainly have better things to do! And the King speaks, albeit not the truth: At best, I will be an annotation in history, but a bold one, in gold print.

Embodied in this man is the bad and the good, I am telling you, that goes for everybody, but I don't like his body, though it ain't so bad for his age. First the King was angry, then he was nice to us again. That keeps changing with him. The only thing he never changes is his clean slate. He doesn't write. He twitters. The thinker imputes that he has been the creator of violence, in his first life, which he still spent among the people. Now he has been elevated, no, he levitated himself, in his gilded elevator, all the way into the sky. We wanted him here and then we will no longer want him to be here. That was my fallacy. He is still here. But in case he will be expelled, also with violence, no idea who's supposed to do it, we'll already have become friends with violence, we'll have got to know it by then; we'll like it better and better, we'll have invested our trust in it, in turn no one else will trust us. We haven't yet got to investigate his conduct of life, we are trying, we only see what he is showing us, maybe we'll never get rid of him, though I don't think that's what he has in mind and whatever is on his mind will happen. But when the time has come, when he might actually be expelled by us and all of humankind, among whom no one would be willing to endure such long-drawn-out investigations, which won't do any good anyway and which he will personally stop at some point, then he'll continue to roam around, at his leisure and pleasure, in his bathrobe, which he doesn't have, in the one house he doesn't own, yes indeed, and he'll also collect himself at times, for collecting is his greatest joy. That is, he will want to make his losses, I think he was winning only as King, now he'll be back counting his losses, losses everywhere, because the losses from realty attractivities, no, activities when the income from other sources, like the springs that wash away the golf courses, something they shouldn't be doing, the springs, our real resources, not the courses, they are just for play, what do I want to say, I don't know yet again, okay, so when the losses climb–in their rubber booties—over and above those springs, our sources which haven't bubbled so profusely else-where, then, well then, the realtors, the kings in their field while ours is the King of All, those then can file an income that is below zero, result: No taxes. Why am I even saying this, it's like that all over the world, when losses exceed earn-ings, then one is a zero. Period.

The King, yes, what did I want to say? Will he first appear to us as a sort of savior?, but then we will let him free again, so he can proceed and hide his proceeds, better than right now, oh yes, our King, well, I'll be curious how the net and all that twitter and the Book of Faces with all its pretty pic-tures, among them sadly none of me, will take to it. Well, because the book takes everything and everyone, and each one in turn takes pictures of others, click, click, click! Thus this book grew and still keeps growing. No one has to look at the King anymore, the pictures are enough for where we live, he prefers living elsewhere. And his tweeting is enough, his cock gets to roost someplace else. He certainly has enough buildings. Oh well, I have no monopoly on the truth, I just play it, can't pay for it, with what, since I only produce losses, he thinks, it's better being king than beggar, I owe the bank so much these days, no repo man could dig up that much gold in my towers, no German repo trooper, it's the Deutsche Bank after all, where we produced them. *Halt*! German!, altright!, the Deutsche, where I have these gigantic debts, but once I'm liquid again I'll buy up the truth or lease it, depending on what's the better deal, I'll buy it on credit like everything else, and I'll also make promises, because credit is for the pros and cons, well, in any event, a promise of more, why should I not take on more debts, and you bet I'll be able to take care of them. And high expenses are also necessary until one earns zero, that's hard work, expenses, they have to be worked up, it takes quite an appetite, expenses are expanding, so are evasions. But people don't turn away from someone like that, quite the opposite, it always comes out zero. Earnings zero. Says he, for the King can afford anything, even zero earnings to—let's say—make it come out in the wash, earnings minus zero, and the least of his worries are his debts. The multiplication of bread is not considered unnatural by him, by none of us who'd like more of it. It started back then, so, when then?, back then, whenever, it started that money was never where it should have been, it always wandered around looking for a new master. The King has the money, that's good, it makes him independent, a big advantage, well, this is why we elected him and God as well has chosen him for it. He is choice. Or rather prime: time. He gets people to take their life, if they still have it and haven't yet had it, into their own hands, but it is an alien life, it is a monstrous man-child they brought along and now you are fucked. This tax return has our signature, but it isn't us, it wasn't us, the man-child you are now holding in your hands wasn't it either, God, is it ugly!, it can't possibly be ours!, it can't possibly be our signature, we had nothing to do with this tax return, the King must have sheltered it under his roof, where he enters with all sorts of gentlemen, enters, enters and exits, oh Lord, I am not worthy. And the creditor isn't happy either when something is missing again. He should actually get compensated—he might have invested this money in something better, in something different, had he only known before what he never knew. They are already lined up at the hairdresser, the bankers, the King gave them the address, they are already in line, they often asked the King, because he is so attractive, where they could get such a reasonable haircut, a similar one like his. What's left—what?, what left?, who, what is left?, whatever, something must always be left, that's the tribute due to the King to finish off, one always owes him something, he does not owe us anything. He owes the Deutsche Bank, *Sieg heil!* One has to be big and be able to think big. Debtors can be locked up, but first we help the people, that's most important. We help them incur debts for starters, their wallets are teeming with plastic and the King didn't come away empty-handed either, he got away with becoming King, what no one expected of him. Does it really matter, for what he uses the money he borrowed? It sure does. But nothing can be done about it. The expenditures are expansive, but they are not based on facts. As mentioned earlier, he did build this wonderful gigantic house, in the middle of somewhere, the only place there is, albeit not for his voters who are everywhere, the main thing is: elsewhere, they'll realize how good that is for them, and now he owes us his life, many home-owners have done it that way, debts and forward march! But before we can take it, his life, he takes ours. Our life gets sucked into a vacuum, which occurs when nothing is left for us and everything is on the other side, where fat asses weigh down the seesaw, and while we weigh ourselves down, because we don't have anything left to throw our weight behind, we are already hurled into the air and then suctioned out like unloved fetuses, whose stem cells no one needs, whose stock, nonetheless, will not die out, on the contrary. There are more and more of us. The poorer, the more. And others are to follow. There really should be fewer people, yet there are more and more, while they have less and less. I also request tax relief. Why does no one grant it to me?

Relieved of their little capital, many more people on your side end up on the see-saw, the first ones are already falling off again, even though the seesaw hasn't moved for eons; don't think it's going up and down, then up again, it only goes further and further down, and that is where they stay, they've been there so long they are beginning to make themselves at home there, even though they no longer have a house, and they have no choice either, even though they voted. All this is not happening in eternity, as you might think, it's happening right here, here or some other place where I've never been. I am beating around the bush, because I got my foot stuck in it so often, at some point I remembered that the system is everlasting and we must put ourselves at the mercy of the bench whose judgment is never the last, or we'd finally be rid of them, at least at the point when we've got nothing. The King also has nothing and look what he made of it! A palace! Countless palaces, well now, they certainly can be counted. That'll never end or it would be the court's last judgment, which we'd notice because we'd never see the day anyone could go through all those files, though we'll hardly last that long. Kindly permit me to make money from nothing, then I'll personally dissolve what is still bonded and bind what is still separate. The Desert. Precisely. There you can't even separate one grain of sand from the other. And you can make losses in unlimited amounts, nobody will notice. It won't cost you anything either.

Now the king is showing his face, really, that's him?, true it is not, I mean, it is not his true face. Nothing he shows is true, it's only borrowed, but he'll never give it back. You can see it already, I don't yet, it is the same as on his King's driving license, which gets him in anywhere, yes, gladly also into women, into every house by way of monitor or a display, he simply gets in everywhere. And then he announces whom he wants to hurt today and whom tomorrow and day after tomorrow, he says: at this time, but that can change quickly, there's something else: I want to hurt neither you or you (he points into the air, but nobody is there). What, becoming my father's murderer? Never! He's been dead for a long time. And if I wanted to kill someone else, it's nobody's business. And if I am friends with people who have killed many, it's nobody's business. It does not faze the King. While I am stubborn to be sure, —I was not begot by someone else, in case you forgot, so help you God, or I would not have become King, right?, no?, well, I would not deny my father, who gave me something to start out with, the others I do, but a homebirth, a self-birth?, well, no, that would be bullheadedness which I don't see for now. Killing the father? We don't believe it! You must believe it, because that's how it goes. And it's been going on for a very long time. A miracle it still stands up, though it is not a laughing matter. What?, no, the father is not standing here. Killing him? I'd never do that, besides, he's dead anyway, how often do I have to repeat that? I'd never do anything that hasn't already been done by many and tried out by real-estate pros, if anything, I'd do it better. Really? Is that true? Or is it just because nobody must know about it? No, everyone should know about it. You too. You must believe that all of them are still alive, the sons, the daughters, you too, the father. Thus, messing with one's mother means just a pleasant bonus once the father is gone and the mother becomes available. A pity she's so old already! The King rather messes with one or more younger ones. Thus he breaks—with the left hand—the myth as well, he breaks up everything, marble, stone, steel, concrete, yes, all of it with the right hand, which is stronger. His Polish workers with their hammers break the rest, I am not trumping this up, it's so unbelievable, no one would believe it. They practically were not or hardly paid. The King always flees screaming shrilly when it's time to pay.

So they are standing over there, and in this photograph, yes, take a look at this tiny device, it would be too small for your head, like the helmets for the Poles at the construction site, that's why they don't get any. I'll just swipe it so it won't slip away, it shouldn't disappear but rather come up, and on this one you can view yourself and her, though I ask myself with what? With your blind eyes? Something like that they can always see! There they suddenly look hard and hot for it, blind or not! But standing over there is someone else, he is like all the others and says he also is a seer, also blind, of course. Way to go! You can deduct it from his account, his eyes have already been written off from his taxes, he deducted himself and then he abducted himself, not as King!, Donald ducked but then he rose again. Oh, human-kind, redeem yourself!, your life, how must I deem it as akin to Nothing, says the King. Let's hope I'll earn this year as little as I keep hearing—one symbolic dollar, so that nothing can be done with regard to finance, that it is zero as usual. Looking at him, there is no one I praise as one blessèd on earth but him. It is the conclusion I draw, which others also draw, no worries, this does not mean the end of it. I can believe that this is what you want, I also want a lot of things, but get nothing! There never was an end to anything with me, I would have to descent into madness were I to believe it. You, King, yes you, who, aiming beyond all measure still hit the mark, you did it, you, entitled to the rapture of power and now you don't want it, handing it over to others to do the work, everyone's working except you, giving the power to others, they are standing around you, one is writing something here, another there, wishing to communicate. And here I stand, no, not a virgin, but with arched claw, I, singer of sooth, banging out bogus, watch out, or you'll be hit by what I banged against before, so that this beautiful statue could rise instead of getting wrecked with sledgehammers. Wreckage must always precede the erection of a high-rise, which is quite big. Throwing off ballast was my way of trying to help my country, but okay, if not, not. I, virgin, I also just wanted to help spreading the song, no, not virgin but everything else is correct, cross my heart, or was it a God who took me, virgin, from the field, me, the true queen, only nobody knows it? No, no God. He wanted this ruler to rule Thebes now, go figure!, yep, but Thebes it ain't, maybe a modern Thebes?, whatever, no God, whom I wouldn't believe in anyway, had wanted that. Believe me! Well, then, believe whomever you want to believe and incur a paper loss, no, there's plenty of paper I won't prevent you from losing.

Oh God, the sacrifice is in a crisis. The cult isn't what it used to be either. Each seer sees something else, that's something to think about, but nobody's got to think just because he can't see. He has other organs he can contemplate, elsewhere. They aren't his. Of course not. But these here are his buildings, of course, the King's got enough of them, that is, plenty of buildings, he just bought another one, buildings are his life, his sustainment, his entertainment, if they have casinos inside. When the payment is past due, it doesn't mean it won't arrive or stay away, it'll just come late, a deed will be recorded, when he pays, our Mr. King, nothing gets recorded. Accepted. Done deal. That's how we do it. The

King is liable for his properties, well, no, let's say he is liable to hang on to hanging on to his properties, to each one of them even if he got it for next to nothing, it's still worth something, the banks will know how much. Okay, King, here are 10 million, that's 2 million more than the purchase price, I'd call that more than generous, it is God's work!, the Devil's contribution are 2,800, in cash. Better than nothing. He ridicules the price he paid for this building, yes, he can laugh his ass off, it's a wonderful building and so cheap!, the furniture alone is worth that much, even more. Yes, but the upkeep, a fortune, the upkeep costs a fortune, laments this man, as he gets into the driver's seat, keeping an eye on the loopholes of the law on his ways around the IRS. What trust is legally due to him according to his claims? Showing off is uncalled for here, better to show less rather than more. With all that windfall the King has got from the bank, he keeps whining about the upkeep, which adds up to more than the value of all that junk. So what. Oh, that you humans feel no shame! But why should we be ashamed, he did not set fires nor paid for murders, thus we chose him in full possession of his powers, but he not us. Now that he has taken a look at us, he seems to want to become King after all. For now he gives up the helm of his buildings and takes everything, winner takes all, the banks are left standing, their legs are almost transparent from starving so much. Not a crumb from the King. The people are leaving their fields before the king pays for anything he bought. You should be ashamed! I have no idea whom I mean. Why should we be ashamed, say the kids. They don't see the trouble in store for their clan.

Everyone sees and says something else, I mean, looks inside himself, since out doesn't work and he says something else, I say: The King will fall, but only because he wants to and when he wants to. He will give up everything and only want to be King. He won't give up anything and still become King. He wanted to know it even at the price of vision and flashlight, but shining outward does not replace the eyesight needed to examine hundreds of beauty queens as to their substance, this one's got nothing to show, same here, that one there much too fat, one is out, some more are out, the King stays. Well, at least it would be good for ruling, the power of eyesight. The word is not his forte except on the telephone where he speaks as someone else with an unfamiliar name. He'll still rule even without eyes, only with his voice and get many, many more votes to boot, he sees everything though he is eyeless, yes and he is also talking, he woos us for our votes, he needs our voices, because his is not his own. So he needs ours. He must be elected, otherwise he sees no future, otherwise he does not see the future. Oh, humankind, what nothing it is, your life, the Nothing, always for me!, Nothing, this way, Nothing, please come to me!, and then they even say something that's different from what they saw, the blind, they assert something and no one dares to contradict, they claim this and that, everyone something else. Because they couldn't see it, so they couldn't see it coming and calmly come to an agreement among themselves either. For it will take place in the future, which is taking place now, but also tomorrow, which is also the future, it's all future and today is almost over.

It's always the same, one and the same. No future whatso-
ever will take place I think, yes, this is what I think. This
Nothing constitutes a lifetime achievement award, he can
frame that or stick it to others, the King. Now the country
finally awakens, it is no longer the Land of the Whites, it is
split as never before, where is this crack, pray tell, we don't
want to fall into it, we want to be either here or there, to the
left or the right of the chasm and look into it and be terrified,
it's dark there, getting darker and darker, this land is our land
no more, it no longer belongs to the Whites, horrible!,
whose is it then?, I don't know, there are so many, I can't
oversee it, let's hope enough cement gets delivered before
we are broke, says the King, so that the house is finished
before we are insolvent. Other towers have fallen, even
though they'd been paid off, this tower shall rise before it no
longer pays to pay it off; yes, indeed, the King's victory is the
best news in centuries, well, let's say, in some time, where
did he go now, the ruler? We can't find him at the moment,
but we find him terrific. Just a few more steps and you'll see
the future for the blind, there it is, we didn't even have to
look so carefully, we would have seen it right away! The one
for seers is always behind them, because it is hard for the
seers to orientate themselves, therefore they don't know
where in front is. They are completely disoriented, even
though they have organs to see. However, they could recognize—if they wanted to—by the headlights which are
installed in front and light up the future up them, where all
this will lead to, and unlike the poor blind people, they don't
need a leader, but they are getting one.

They foresaw that someone else would soon be sitting on the throne, I could have told you so right away. A new time passed them by, which had moved away already at their birth. But we know its address. Make contact, quick, the new time has already begun! Hurry up or you won't get in! And yet, behind the dead eyes of the seers and behind the backlights of the seeing and the televisionaries, where the nations interweave, and I in the middle of it, I am locked in there with all the others, something could play out there, which is no longer just play. They have to turn around constantly, which does not help them, like the Angel of History, whom I drag in every time I can't think of anything else. If you want to stick it to him, you have to buy an envelope that really sticks together and lick it and send it or don't. You have the choice. You don't even get near the Angel, if you don't want to co-determine the fate of your country. Go ahead, take this ruler, he is quite sticky, though you may be the one to get licked. He is not blind, but very terrified that loans get terminated, though this never happens or banks would plummet screamingly into the construction pit and on principle he always looks in the wrong direction, to where you are not. And he doesn't even owe you. You wouldn't be worth it for him being indebted to you, you have nothing to give but your voice, but that's what he has himself, one or more voices, more voices by different names when he makes telephone calls to accomplish something he could not accomplish as a human. Yes, and anyone who just doesn't see will have to wait a bit anyway. For those we have a special program, a kind of limbo after which they definitely get it, they get to see everything except the King's tax return. It says it all, I mean it says that nothing gets out, no, it says that it says nothing about tax liability, well, forget liability, but that he will keep lying to the country. The King is never liable, he is always only right. Say what? Yes, well, go ahead, say it!, what do you mean? That a future is happening and you are doing well, you are well off, especially as white race you are very well off, by and large, aren't you? So tell me, who then is supposed to do all the work? Oh, right, we also have the Polacks and the bean-eaters, they work for 'well,' that is, for nothing. They work well, but get nothing. And world trade? Also doing well? The nations get locked out, and they respond: With what? What do they say to it all? This race will lead into the abyss? Is this the crack from before? Did I get into the wrong one? The globe is hardly recognizable! Okay, so it is happening, the stupid future, so be it, I won't live to see it anyhow. This one knows them and greets them and hands out his prizes, no, prices, he'll call his union man again tomorrow, with that guy he doesn't have to disguise his voice, ouch, another paycheck just bounced. So take the present into account, where Jimmy Hoffa has disappeared, no, he disappeared in the past, the union man shakes his head slowly and suggests that one could notify the office of the confederates, no, the federates, those workers are illegal, to be fired on the spot, the whole kit and kaboodle! At least it will get warm on the construction site, I don't care, but before that I'll use every opportunity to make money, by not letting anyone else earn anything. Thus everything remains with me. That King! Hell bent, he, and out of shape, especially his crown of hair, beware! What a bitter life that from now on he too must live among humans and as their Führer to boot, not very flattering having to lead such people, he'd prefer others. But there he is, the King. What gatherings of citizens will he attend, what parties, which many will leave crying but don't want to, they want to stay and participate. Participation is all. What misery are we still missing? Maybe he'll tell us. So now he wants to secure the future with debt-financed expenses! It already didn't work for the many single-family homes, but maybe the country can sustain something like that and then we are all financed and don't have to worry anymore, because we can finance everything with our debts, a boundless boon, if we can also buy the neighbor's property, that's what the guy there is saying and also that one over there, many are saying it whose income stagnates and will soon have to start burglarizing.

And coming along now is even a woman with some kind of claws, no, it's not the sphinx, even though one might think so, because she sings, the bitch, she sings, for a change she is not a seer, she just knows, she knows, no need for her to understand—no seer, she, or she would have the self-blinded King staggering around right in front of her eyes, because he can't find the mirror, for he can see himself only there, even blind he knows his way in the mirror, that potted narcissus, and he is beside himself, no, beside himself he doesn't want to see anyone—she knows—she, who is not a seer at all, knows who will soon be sitting on the throne, but we all know that and are desperate! Blood comes out of the woman's eyes, that's what comes out if one confides to a woman, this one, however, does not trust us, blood is shooting out of her, from wherever, I almost assume also from below, that is, from everywhere. And she claims she can see the future, but that's only her claim. She has also been financed by our debts, as are most things here, and the rest we also pay with our debts. But there is nothing left, the King used up everything, so now he could use us. Okay with me. I ask you, what good is a seer for—if he wants to be a woman, why not seerina, now that really was unnecessary, even our native seers say so—if he couldn't see the future, if he could only overlook, I mean oversee, whatever, what's going on these days? *Heil! Heil!* to our *Volk!* Rise and once again, louder: *Heil!* Please do not mock this blind Führer, it's not his fault that he is blind. Let's rather have this woman. No, not that one, she'd rather stay at home, can't do much worse there. She'd rather get herself a new body and new face and then another one and then again another one. We appreciate women. Now we appraise them. It wasn't always like this, when we only appreciated models, whom we never met, especially those. Yes, very especially those. We only claimed we knew them and more than knew them. She says no, but not to the King. Doesn't matter. Women for the King, yes, that one there and this one too, but actually it was only one, something the King wants to veil, instead of veiling all the other women, saying he doesn't want those, who'd want to look at that. It says so on this screen, so it is transparent. What does a stranger know? What does a blind man see? What could he do to those dwelling in the light? Looking at it in the light, I'd want a new dwelling right away.

We have been pulled into the game and bet on ourselves for many millions, no, we rather bet on the millions, our chances are bigger then. We are not above any conflict, we create the conflict. And the wise guys who will enter now are not blind, they are in a blind rage, they are not wise, they are wild, which fogs up their brains, they don't even recognize the cave where their camp is and pitch it wherever they like. They are forever and everywhere, there are ever more of them, more and more new ones keep coming. But what will hurt most in all this misery—it will turn out to be self-chosen. Lately the blind are called advisors, that's not as discriminating. Oh most honored men of this country—the women and every-thing in-between are of course also meant by the term—I have great respect for them, for all, bar none, everyone, men-o-men, what deeds will you hear of, see or not see, what pain will you feel? If we want to wash this house afterwards again, we will have to divert the whole river, otherwise it won't get clean. But what will hurt the most about all this pain is that it will turn out to be self-elected.

So, have we all had it now? No, you just have it coming, a second coming, a tradition everyone knows already anyway. The cave we live in is quite small, everything can be seen even by a blind man, a seeing one can look at it as writing on the wall, and those who dwell with us are asked right off what stock they come from. They say they don't know stock from Adam, but they still rule like a king, until they get freed again?, even though they just elected one, whatever. Mean-while, the historical stock, i.e. tradition, has been traded,

disguised as that which has been and will be at the same
time, elected is elected and thus the past we overcame came
over us like the plague that's curative, no, curable, why did
it come at all?, what for?, to decide for, over us? To perform
this tradition, to wit, the eternal, it has to put on a new costume that will last a bit longer, maybe all the way to heaven's
gate, because here on this land it can never be eternal, here
it must be harvested. It won't make it; won't it, really? A tradition cannot be altered retroactively, otherwise it would be
an oracle that's known for being right in only half the cases;
so the overcome arrogates to itself the move, with all its
uncreative pomp, into this house only, which the ruler hasn't
even built himself, who would even want to move in there?,
but people almost kill each other for it, well, I say uncreative,
since what came over us has long been here already, it might
seem done in, but it is far from done, it is the old we already
know and are now permitted to welcome as new, because it
is always necessary to get a new person, even in one's own
family. Thus we are told and we must accept this disgrace:
being like everyone else. The King, at any rate, can't stand
being like us. We are afraid of the new, it will never belong
to us, nothing belongs to us anymore anyway!, what more
leasing rates could there be?, how many of us can be consumed as workers without consumer protection, which the
King does not grant us, what for?, he doesn't need it either.
We are still waiting for what the overcome has come to arrogate to itself, just that one house mentioned before, that's
not enough for us, there must be higher grounds for it, we
haven't yet said for what and how all this came to be!, it

should at least be coming now!, we said a lot, but not this, right? It should be saying it right here, and you would have to name it, at the top of your voice, shouted down from this platform, does it arrogate this arrogation or not, or something else that'll suddenly come over us? Well, then just about anyone could come along! We'll never come up with the rates, they got us way in over our heads, we don't even manage to give our wishes a real chance, because they already had their one and only chance. We voted, I didn't, but others did in my place, but they were not where I wanted them, they were elsewhere and made the wrong choice and such wishes must also be paid for at some point. Okay, so now we know more or less what this tradition does, do you?, I wrote this, but I don't know either. The fruit of the globe, no, of globalization are finally distributed as unfairly as possible, the disaffected grow on trees and get picked and processed into juice, that yields more than eating them raw, because for juice the mushy and rotten ones can also be used. The doings of tradition, who cares?, well, you don't know it, but I, I at least have an idea, I just can't say it, so then what does the overcome, no, that what's coming over us really do, we'd very much like to know, at least now?, and you still owe it to us, we don't like debts all that much, the banks are more likely to. Then they can really slap it on, and we'll be the ones to get hit. Move over there please, that's where you'll get it.

No wonder we've been abandoned and don't even have wishes anymore and have cut off our own words. Well, Ms.

Author, you produced a lot of words for this. I haven't known for a long time what I'm saying, but the King doesn't know either. He says it with a forked tongue, one never knows which half says what. His workers must rip the cables out of the wall with their bare hands, I wouldn't dare to do that and they are not even permitted to wear respiratory masks! Why do they need to protect their breath!, they need it for something else. It wasn't me who made the debts, I assumed them, used!, from someone else, from several people. I don't remember who said that and who left us afterwards, lest we'd find him, it must have been someone else again! Even if we bypass the backward-turned to get to the front we still have to, unfortunately, look, even if just for a moment, into his white face, we intentionally don't look, we avoid on purpose to look in differently colored faces, for one moment we must see what has been and what's coming, while we can speak—without overstating it—, of what's coming over, no, coming down on, no, condescending to us, all these words are wrong, but we need to choose them, because no others come to mind, so then the condescending and its friends, yes, each one like a gun we carry on our shoulders, we carry it all the time, everyone can carry it, that's what we are fighting for!, it can start any moment, anyone can carry it, like the saint the Christ child, through the river, I know he became a saint only later, because neither one drowned, so let's wait, the overcome, here it is again, without us knowing what it's supposed to serve, but serve it must, welcome!, we know you, don't we?, we even know your friends! You bet!, we hump it, no, we'll hump it to the dump; no, wrong place; the overdone, note, I said overdone, not overcome pomp, what's with it, you've been talking about it all this time, do you even know what pomp is? No? At least I know what a punk is. Please, no more bad pomp, I mean, pun. Well, I don't know, it's worth some reflection, albeit not mine, someone else reflected upon it who—in this respect as in every other—commands far more respect than I, doesn't matter. Okay, so, the overcome arrogates, in the unconsciousness of its calculations, which always come out wrong, because it makes no sense to calculate something in an unconscious state, I can't even count when I am in my right mind and not out of it, I always digress, I beg your pardon, it already happened for the tenth time at least, Herr Heidegger is to blame, for once I am addressing him personally now, because many times he has served me well, inasmuch as I misunderstood him: What's got in your mind, which absolutely no one else would have got? I don't yet even understand what I could misunderstand.

So there has been counting and calculating and the outcome is, that one, the number one, the one and only, he, with his wealth, his whims he can afford—please come to an agreement on who that's supposed to be, because here he is, he's already standing at the door, no, he is inside now—that this very one has been looking for freedom, but picked the wrong door and now he is one hundred percent yours. Or was that another one? Oh, I see, you've already agreed on the one, in order to talk about his empowerment, I won't do it again, well, now, this mindless capitalizing of the historical customs which haven't yet been delivered to the capital, they were too new, those costumes, but will get quickly distressed, no, sorry, I keep forgetting: Here he is!, the King, everything has happened already, but isn't over yet. Or will it only begin to happen, or is it currently happening elsewhere, in another dimension?, no, in ours, a rare event, so one can see already what is (but so far it is not yet, so far it is nothing), so for now let's thoroughly absorb this during the vote count. Did the slot machines lie? They can cause you pretty big losses, by the way. Has someone else thrown in something or taken something out? Let's be glad for the input, a putt that gets the ball rolling, not to confuse with a put-on what many could think it is, the game is on, one can't see the gamer and there is no one there to catch the ball. Maybe he thought it was just an old ballot and threw it in the wastebasket? Whatever. He would have wanted more and more. But it already was enough. What have we done? The seer wants messengers to report to him and then he'll lie and say he saw it himself. But the messengers have the wrong app and the wrong handicap and they see that we voted for the wrong guy, but there is nothing they can do. They are reportable to the advisory council, but, who can't be counseled can't be helped. Now nobody knows what he should do. Well, for starters he must confirm in writing that he is not a computer, no, he isn't, a bot would bet on a different picture, this here shows beyond any doubt a human, a real one, but as for his voice, doubts are advisable and even this picture is very telling, but no one has the key to it.

Not too much correctness, no screaming, no spitting, no picketing, no window smashing, no screaming *HALT*! STOP! at every opportunity, that'll stop nothing!, not people who won't even brake for animals! No accusing others of being stupid! That applies to me, I do it all the time. No looking down on others! No rising and if so, leave the chair on the ground! No self-righteousness, no correctness, but nothing either that could offend or hurt others. If disappointed do not be disappointing yourself. In any case, no misleading others. The King says what's what, only you are always deluding yourself, not the King. Best not to be at all, this is what already Herr Egger taught his Heidis and Adis to recommend to those Jews whom he would never have wanted for his son-in-law, though this goes just for Germany, otherwise, the Jews can actually be quite practical: Either to be or not to be at all. Who knows what ploy the ruler has in mind for us, he's always working on ploys and he also employs workers who must pay union fees from their meager wages, even though no one represents them. No pay for overtime, that goes for you too. What, you already know? What do you know? You can't say, but you know it. Because you are talking with anyone, even with people you want to punch in the mouth, you already know it? You were lucky. He didn't say a word and walked off, you foresaw this? What did he say, what did he look like, how was his gaze? Did he speak at all? Clearly? In his right mind? Conscious of it?

We don't do such things. We don't overlook others. They are too big for us. But we can't believe the result, it must have been rigged. Okay, one can see what is, but what does it do?, what is it up to now?, a few more subordinate clauses, please, then maybe you'll forget the beginning, the one about scum, no, cum—oh, come on now!—Sorry, come it is: the overcome (the translator for one!, what with the past, the passed on past, the hand-me-downs, the coming down on all of us: TRADITION!), okay, so then, the overcome, if I am lucky, if not, then Heidegger was lucky when he wrote it in the Black Notebook. A lot gets written by a lot, but you must not despise them, not criticize them, not terminate a loan, anything that's not the case and where there is nothing and nothing ever happened. Don't not, never, despise others!, also very important. No monopolizing the truth, look at it first if it's worth buying it. Look, you might need it to last for a lifetime, so it's worth you owning it and not only all the stuff you are likely to have heard somewhere without liking it. Who are you anyway? You think, you are the only one living in the light? Other people also have a current flowing through their home. Yes, let's just besmirch, what has made us so great and the others ever smaller! What? So, go ahead, booh, the worst is yet to come at the end, where it doesn't fit, so then, once again from the start: The historical stock, tradition—That which came over us, just a moment, do I seriously mean this or am I more serious about the overcome, that is that, which—well, whatever, I think it's neither the overcome nor the passed on, since no one has ever seen such a thing, it must have disguised itself, since we don't recognize it under that egg-yolk-yellow blow-dry coif, a fine coif, by the way, very delicate, almost transparent, a spook, no, a spoof—at least you might think so, you wouldn't recognize anyone under such a hairdo, or, rather, only one single one and that's not you, much less the one I'm talking about, he doesn't even want to look like that, but has to, yes, he, it's him I mean, you don't even really look at him!, even though he always stays the same, except on the telephone, there he is one or several others. There he fakes his voice, that's proven, there are witnesses, he fakes himself until the man on the other end feels totally fucked, the conversation is finished, thank you for the conversation. That is the royal way. Or is it a way of calculating, that did not immortalize, but rather disguised itself out of the historical stock? Whatever, we recognize it nonetheless, because it's always the same, whether disguised or handed down in the original, we recognize it any which way, because it's the good old ways, because it stood the test of time. No, we always want something new, but we know that the old is good, because it has proven itself. We want change, we want to charge with the change, finally something new, it can't go on like this, but what we really want is, that the good old hand-me-downs are now the new thing, so that we recognize it. And the old is always good or still good, we understand that you prefer it to the new, we shouldn't criticize you for it, even though millions died of it and still others made millions in the King's casino, always good, good enough to bring out and recount who or what is missing or came along to return this new thing that's been promised to us and make it great again, greater than it has never been. *Heil*!

What to do, so that tradition, that stock-in-trade, that passed on past, that sorry hand-me-down, DAS ÜBERLIEFERTE, damn you, Honeg—NO, Heidegger!, (but that's the end of it now, okay?! Don't know yet) can get away as new again? It gets away with it again and again, but it doesn't get new, watch out, it bolts!, there, it's disappearing in the distance!, we can't grasp it, because it ran off once again, it did not run off with us, it simply ran off, because you, the masses, howling, hollering, whistling, made room for it, but in the wrong direction, *Heil!*, he won't be running there for sure. He always wants to go somewhere else and get something else, so that it can project, reflect the new. The King is blind and this mirror is blind too. Can't find out anything through it. The mirror says nothing. You can leave out all there was, it no longer means anything to us. Anything true is gone anyway. Do you dwell in the light, are you in the picture? Not much longer, just between you and me. The mountains howl, the bays howl after you because they did not think of it. And you can't just throw my word back in my face either! Where would that get us!

The elect who was elected by enablement, is already behind you, he is no longer a forerunner, he is a rearkicker, no, a reargunner, no, that he ain't for sure, we do have proof of that, two or three proofs, they could even live in the tower free of charge, they were all women, that is, of the female sex, and let their gorgeous hair down until the prince came and declined when he saw the rest. Just because you don't see him doesn't mean he's got to be far ahead of you, maybe he'll also come to you, just wait a little, he might come, at least he'll claim that he has come, but didn't want to stay. He and women! Something hot is cooking here, but he doesn't want anything solid right now, he doesn't get it anyway. Once he decides, he'll make a woman very happy, now don't blame me, that's what's been handed down, but not even everything you read in the Bible is all true. He hasn't yet decided, please, don't feel deeply duped, you are not. And neither are you, don't be dashed to the ground, there is no more room, too many other victims are lying around there. But he could easily also be far behind you, then he's breathing down your neck. Either way he simply loves to lead, did he make all this up just to show off as a playboy? I don't know, I only see that he is having an affair, as he boasts. Boastfulness is next to godliness, but it also comes at a price. At some point the King no longer leads, because he's already led on everyone, but never kept a single woman in tow, except one, he says, his rope tore off or he would have got all of them, he's only got a few more to go. Instead he's leading now, the whole country is his alone to lead, on and on and on, no longer does he depend on anyone, no longer must he care about a deposition from anyone. He is in the position to depose anyone. How about you? Do you need leadership? Yes, you do, that's what you voted for, and you got a leader who knows how. Now women are only his second favorite secondary matter. The country from now on will be his main thing, it gets annexed to his other properties. *Heil!* Did I treat this serious topic humorously? No idea. I tried.

Well, here I have the first proposition, no, not of the law of thermodynamics, which is about a closed system, wherein energy remains the same at least until one takes stock of the energy and discards the lightbulb, something like that. His: always positive. The balance is always positive, even when he's got nothing. There's something about him that seems more than he has. Dynamic. Since we are at it, though we aren't with it, at least our thoughts are somewhere else: As for me, sadly there's nothing dynamic about me, I cooked up this first sentence which can't be closed, no one could close it because you just disclosed you decided something else, it doesn't work, it simply stopped working, it went on for so long, but it won't go further; I use my rack and o-pinion, what's the outcome? The sentence moves in a totally different direction, where it can be milked until the milk prices sink permanently, which will never happen. I can't do it, let alone produce energy, no, I am not able to say what I want to say, what I am saying, no, even that is not my saying, a law of nature asserts it: Man will, even if he bleeds from everywhere, from above, from below, out of the center, even if he is a woman, even if he is an adversary, what, of whom?, even if he is himself, whatever, that battle is over and decided, man will turn into dirt, and it won't even pay off for him if a bomb is let loose; he doesn't even get paid, after all. The developers will take care of that. Those pushing ahead piss on everything, those retreating piss off to take a leak somewhere, they leak a lot of shit, a real dump. Just recently I saw one of those again, Dixi, my favorite. The simple tolerates nothing, it does not tolerate any historical accounting, because it is singular. The simple abjures the complex, it is inexhaustible, the simple and what does it demand? It demands the most difficult: being able to return to the same. Thus meeting each other are those who want to get ahead, and those who push backwards, they meet on the battlefield where a wild dog stands, heckling, that's all that's left, there is nothing in-between. And the truth hides, yes, that's nice, the truth hides from those who hide themselves, like a gust of wind that blows away the earth in a remote valley bottom in the Black Forest or wherever the earth will soon be gone with the wind and yes, so that folks who meet smack in the middle and bash in each other's their skulls, might realize in one blink of the eye their kinship and then, for a moment or perhaps another blink remember God, because they can't think of anyone else and He considers people quite useful, big deal, he made them, he just doesn't quite know what for. Why am I saying this now? But I'm not saying it! Or too often. All the time! They calculate and calculate themselves out of their minds, those human projections, they are available everywhere, even in highest resolution, which, however, also dissolves quite swimmingly, that's the disadvantage of resolutions in high places. Those who can swim might even get the right to stay, though not in the water, where there are fishes and dead bodies. God imagined it differently, somehow more solid, well, so be it. At least they are somewhat decimated. They calculate something, those left ashore do, but not those left behind, because they can calculate only in a state out of their minds, I can't do it either way, no matter in what state, because that stupid blood keeps running out of my eyes, whenever I want to see something that's far ahead of me.

Okay with me. So here's the out-of-mind calculation: hello, please put on this costume, with it you can disguise yourself as a historic custom, to use a different term for that handed-down stuff, or let's call it something inherited, so we can say it's something that was delivered to us as our historic deliverance—that is something inherited we had never seen before, the costume with all that pomp, I am not saying the pompous costume, though that's what it also is, I mean the one with the fake, because uncreative pomp and circumstance of the world-viewer, the worlds-viewer, who does not want to see the world, it doesn't matter to the one who classifies the world as to where he can build or where he can ram golf courses into the ground, oh well, I am exaggerating again on the one side and I exaggerate on the other, but as King he has to take a look at the whole world. Why can't you see what stood there before you slapped down your tower there? He can no longer see it, he is inside the tower. No kidding! You've got to look up to this high-rise, first you have to go out, then look up, then you can see it, then you see him, way up high, having a blast at the very top, but it will also come down on us underlings, he will come down to us and blast us to pieces. He sees it, he doesn't see it, but he knows it is there and it belongs to him. How come he is the only one who sees it?, because he is blind?, no, seeing does not work at all, because he is inside and from there he can't see the top and fancies that he himself is the top, yes, he is over the top! And this overcome having overcome us—I can't believe I am still coming up with this!!, it assumes this superiority, which is a sham. Here a sentence comes to an end, whose beginning had several starts and it even ended several times, it still remains in the dark. I can't believe it finally departed, it is so disparate, nobody wanted it, (and the translator was desperate), because it went on and on and on, most of you have left already, I am asking for respect for it, it wanted to think first and then say something orderly. Not everyone can make this claim. Don't disturb the silence of the dead. It won't be finished, the sentence. It isn't necessary, the King was often broke and might be now again. Who cares? He least of all. He gets a whole country in return, and a big one to boot, so please, don't be sad! We let the seers do the seeing! Everyone in his place, forward march!

I, for one, but I cannot vote, I am not eligible, not everywhere I want to and if I could have, I would not have chosen you, I would not have taken you. I'd rather have taken a wet sponge with which I'd have cleaned the world, I don't have to sweep my own small horizon, one breath would be enough, one last breath to cloud it even more, which I did not have in mind to do. It wouldn't have taken a village to lure me away from you, I would have personally taken anyone but you, though I am sure that you won't take this personally, but you: Never! Did you go out with this woman? I'll leave that open. Come on now, you, as your own PR boss must know: Where were you when you went out and with whom? Not even on the deathbed, hers or his would that woman go out with him, says she! She does not say: The best sex I ever had has been with him, but you leave it up in the air with whom. Kept up in the air and in question it is. All of us actually know it by now, it is not true, however. Don't laugh, that's what's been said, it's about a man who makes dishonest business deals, it wasn't me who said that— still, I am saying it—and he didn't say it either, he doesn't say things like that. Forget suing me, the court is already a sewer. It's about a man who cheated on his wife, not this one, the current one but the first one, there was another one in-between, that's a reasonable number, even I can count to three. Go figure if that's not worth a prize for lifelong excellent performances. The King has given it to himself. The question is, will we be able to forgive him when he has blown us up and only the air-conditioner factory remains and as many people as are needed for it, well no, there'll probably be a few less. This book, which you only know by its covers, naturally you haven't read it, you would have closed it, before you even attacked the first few pages. You knew it wouldn't work, you don't like it after all. It would have come out at the inspection. Your money back if you don't like it. One could make good money from your not liking so many. You took many, but this supermodel, you left her out, though you leave that open, you let on just a bit, though it's out in the open anyway. You, after all, have the choice among the most beautiful, which you can take as the main dish or side dish, depending, those who don't even have to put on their coats, but just throw them around the shoulder, who show one shoulder and then the other, because they know how, who show themselves nearly naked, because they can afford to, who can show themselves everywhere, including their legs, only a few belong to those, to those legs, by which everyone recognizes them, so then the one with those legs, only that one, but she already belongs to him, him alone, it's the one he chose, she lives in the tower, in a gold shower, but doesn't stand in the storm, she isn't that great. Are you still following? All told, there were not more than three pieces of women and still he creates such hot air around them, they appear again and again, swaying, wavering, should they choose him or another?, come on, that's not really a choice, here they are, the women, therefore consider their bitter lives' further course; I see blood everywhere, wherever humans must live blood shows up as well. But in no way should it spoil you the cruel bond that chains those two together. How are children supposed to get through it, how should they risk to take such infamy as beset their parents. I don't quite know now how many children, there is only the one who counts and her other one, that is her husband, and that's another story and then two sons and the youngest son, that's quite a lot. Oedipus did not muster as many children as this King. And not even he accomplished it with one single womb, he needed three for it, but then they were there, the children, who all work in his business, in the hotel business. There they don't have to set out on this bitter course and they can always sleep at home. And they will visit the citizens' gatherings, what beautiful, what lovely fests of solidarity those are! And the father too has something solid, not only a firm handshake, which comes absolutely gratis.

Take me, the women tell him, take me, he hears everything, I hear nothing, this one says nothing at all and the other one over there doesn't either. So many women and only three pieces suitable! That's more than nothing, three pieces. How well can the King be equipped, that he creates so much hot air around it and then it all goes down his pants. It's only a talk show anyway. The King lives nowhere else. That's like with God, we know where he lives, up in the penthouse, you see his picture everywhere, you hear his cheery assurances that he has again been assured of something he doesn't have to pay for, that's what we do, friends, hear ye God lest it comes to a hearing! This one, and another, god, whoever it may be lives in a picture that can be brought in and then made to disappear again. This is what is done to the holy body of the King, he is brought in and then put away again. And at some point, when his body has been shown a lot in this tabernacle of shiny gold, no one will want to see him anymore, simply because he is everywhere. He is already here, I wish I never knew him, I don't know him anyway, but there he is, has his big entrance which is indistinguishable from the small ones, the masses of his followers are incalculable, but they don't have to be personally present, no one can be missing when he appears in his device, because there they must see him, whether they want to or not. Those who aren't there can't be seen either. Duh! You've probably never heard anything different, or rather you couldn't ever, that's all beyond the little frame. Three women. Help yourself, take me! He thinks, that's what they tell him. But at least one is saying something else. Around me, the world remains silent, but I scream! Not even when I scream am I heard, for the angels have arranged themselves around God, not us. Born not in the shadow of a pompous palace was I, but everyone would love to let me go from this country.

Always such a show! Applause, Applause, thank you, Kermit! Then take another one, I don't mind, if you like her better!, But she should be like one who is like the other, except you won't find many others, at this price we don't have them in stock, but they'll grow back, because they want to, poor things don't want the calm before the agony of starving. And the country, the dear country? How can it take all this? Trembling with excitement, the dear country enters from the vestibule where it waited, it won't get a view, it's already got it, and it can't contain itself anymore; it's in full view, and do we really want to hear the poorest's lament as to what they lost, houses, albeit small ones, health, albeit not very good, children, not much good either, school?, what's that to be good for?, life?, what life? Trembling with agitation well, almost livid, it comes along, too late as usual, no, this time it is right on the money, the electors are still counting, but they know already what they'll say, if once in their life they'd count. Now how about that, now the country shows up, when it's too late!, it's running to the conjugal chamber, the country, it's one of the big ones, where the new king is waiting already, let's hope it knows what it must do, it has done it so often anyway. With the tips of both hands it tears its hair, which doesn't need it, the country, which does need it, now what?, the King barely has any worth mentioning,

better we don't mention it, but whatever's still there everyone knows, from many jokes, which like any calamity, will
pass, we are past joking; still, his name shall be mentioned
many times, it's not about hair, but what's underneath,
somewhat like the Islamic headscarf and the brain. So there
the country comes shooting into the chamber to the King,
well, I don't want to say it's really shooting, although it
could, so it shoots in to the King, it did not check in, it goes
through by and with itself, the *Volk* itself is the gatekeeper
and it lets itself in to the King, who isn't the one it expected,
the country, and now it bemoans the bed it should lay in, the
bed is made, now it's just got to screw itself, the country, no,
the other way around, the country has voted, now it regrets
it already, it regrets it yet again it voted wrong, the country,
it's been conned, it elected the wrong one; and screaming,
the King rushes in to put it all straight and put on his show;
the vote is in; and still, they hail him, they couldn't do more
than they've done already and yet, they hail him: It's him,
no doubt, he is it!, but then, it's not him either, my God, he'll
offer us all as his sacrifice. He's done so much already, he can
deliver this too, the King, it's all a game for him, not so easy,
not so serious, it is a game the rules of which he doesn't
understand, he doesn't need them, he'd rather have shouted
than said something, it would be like standing as a light in
the dark, similar to my bedside lamp, you have to imagine it
like that, no, you don't have to do anything.

He doesn't know any other way but in, many behind him
who write down for him what he should say, but he can also

blurt out his own thing, and better, why not, but then it is something different from what he's been urgently advised, these are often pretty violent solutions, which, so far at least, only killed the puny pun intended in this clause, sorry, dear author; so the King rushes in as one who has not yet been there earlier, the bed is empty, maybe he was with another woman, in another country, who knows, maybe he found another model, according to whom he would want to reshape women, though not all of them, there always must be opportunities for comparison to realize that the King's wife is incomparably beautiful. The other stupid cunts should nevertheless strive to emulate this role model in case they aren't models already, they are less work then. Then they are form, pure form but which one?; yes, there is content too, but one can't see it, that's for sure, no, not sure, obscure, obscene. Form and content no longer there, with destructive violence we arrive at unanimosity: My way or the highway. Thanks, not necessary to see in me an *über*-natural, no, an unnatural creature. Maybe a counter-natural? Naturally! Nature does want it, but no one else does?, a creature who sows peace to harvest violence?, no, the other way around. That gentleman there, what does he have to say to me, he taunts me, I act like a terrifying but mysterious redeemstress of absolutely everything and should not be performed at all, period.

He laughs at me, yes, the one over there, he can hardly talk, he's laughing so hard, happy to be the cause, and what does he say? He's got to say something, for laughing out loud, that I get all worked up as this mysterious redoomer who makes people sick in order to heal them right after, which I, however, would deny. Besides, people don't have to get healed and if they do, then not by me, it's actually quite reasonable, what the King is saying, isn't it? Now that you say it, it's clear to me. You, Ms. Author, what will you obsess about now? You are still human, aren't you?, you shouldn't try our patience, we already gave you a generous discount for your life and it is getting shorter quite nicely, we are the cause of it, this was granted to you for the price of your sacrifice. You may say what kind of sacrificial victim you want to be, and what kind you want to sacrifice, make sure not to confuse the two! Of course you want to be an innocent victim that gets thrown to some monster or something like that. And I won't say this now, I am just scribbling it, I mean, I ascribe it to me that I myself am at the mercy of the people's revenge or, on the contrary, my desire for justice. So, yes, justice is very important to me. That's what is said here about any sacrifice, albeit also by every victim. Doesn't matter. As a matter of fact, I especially enjoy showing off as the victim.

Our time is up, yes, of course, I also mean mine, don't get upset for no reason, I don't count, but I absolutely count myself in here. There are names for all miseries I described, is one missing? Yes. It's missing and it will be supplied ASAP and in the following order, which I did not think up, unfortunately: groaning and confusion, death and ignominy. I might have more thoughts on this, then I won't have to find names for all the miseries, since we already have names, none of them will be missing, I might miss it, but it won't be missed. For a long time we were right, for a long time we had the right, to push aside the word fear, now it is here and it is here to stay. It glues itself on us like the eyes of love on somebody, because love is even less choosy than us writers, who constantly look into the dark, because it is more interesting to them. The good landlord gave us the key to it, but we haven't found anything yet. You can't see anything, you can invent anything that belongs in it, mean sons kill their fathers, why are they doing this? There is no reason, though it will be explained in detail. The eyes of the father who made you and who we make fun of, so bright before, are trying to look for you, and this is stupid, I don't mean to say because of the monthly guilt and debts, it's just really stupid if someone, not seeing, not asking, clueless, becomes father to children in exactly the same place, where he himself had once been sown. To avoid the guilt and debts that always follow, one should either not beget children, who then have to pay that we even have a chance to get into a nursing home or make sure the planet will collapse, as soon as possible under infinite growth and everyone must pay, it is always the same, not only the father the alimony, which is supposed to secure the future of the children, that is, create hope for them, but in truth the purpose of debts is that all hope for the future should get destroyed and that hopes would be robbed and so on. Isn't Oedipus a beautiful symbol for this? Innocent begetter of promises, two promises even, begotten with his mother, so that at least it stays in the family, who always profited from it, yes, the family always wins, because there are more to them and knocking out hope at the same time, oh well. The impression that anything can be changed is deceiving, it's over.

Now I will, perhaps, describe the King, he is supposed to be indescribably wealthy, I heard, at least money like Midas and has masses of crown corks, with which he keeps hitting the fan. But I am not sure; the banks are groaning, because he is sitting on them instead of entrusting something to them. That one's a grabber, he's a die-hard and now he's got really hard. Finally. He rose early, because incest, no, I can't accuse him of that, that's a no-no, because he would not commit incest with a woman older than thirty-five, that one's dropped. The opponents within the family or those who got there on busses from the outside, since they don't get into his family, there everyone must be beautiful or they are out, but they don't get in and they don't get it, I don't either, really everyone's getting there, because when I participate, it's really everyone, then I am not missing anyone—so all those opponents are beating up on the King, they slam his golfing pants, his gold toothbrush cups, his gold toilet-paper holders, he gets beaten up on, because one would love to be beaten his way, someone like him is still bigger when he gets beaten, bigger than us who are cared for, if only by ourselves and our kind, yes, better to get beaten as King than as a fif-teen-year-old girl by fellow travellers, who are richly equipped with telephones that can film nowadays, by fellows her age, who only hit, so they won't get hit and may grow older. Conclusion: I would prefer you be beaten and not I, no, you cannot click on the video again today, you don't want to anyway, you don't need it either. You do not want what everybody has, after millions already saw it on the net and kept it as their precious treasure, which they play back over and over again, as a remembrance of nothing, of something that did not happen to them, well, wouldn't you say that's how it goes: The King only hits back, he defends himself, everyone may do that, even a minor, even a minion, even a child; so incest is out, but violence, extreme violence always works, the destruction of difference; here I don't mean it like that thinker, whose thinking I happen to have in front of me, but never behind me, because I do not understand him, here I don't mean the destruction of the greatest differences within one family, which all Americans are or whatever *Volk* has the say-so, at the moment it is me, but I am not a *Volk*: the destruction of the main difference in the family is my concern, and not only mine, namely, the destruction of the difference to the mother, but then all of this is not what I mean, it is too extreme for me. Too many dead and one single individual confronting them, one, a king, inside whom everything was extinguished by incest and murder, any need for mother and children simply extinguished, his eyesight, also extinguished just like that, well, it wasn't all that simple, but rather like that famous, devastating death on the cross extinguished something, I can't think of what right now, it must have been something anyway, why would someone take on such a thing?, come on now, one person can't bear all this by himself, sins, family, we know both, no longer have to be self-made, they are already hanging on the wall, written in this book which the King has not or would not have read either before or after his blindness, no, in another book which, alas, he does not know either. So then, with these crimes, these horrible crimes one single individual elevates itself, it immortalizes itself and gets immortalized, versified, perversified, unfortunately not by me. I rather not say what I mean, first blood will have to blend even better for the working class to disappear and rise in us again, as seed or sun, as desired, it is here, but it should not be seen, maybe better as seed, which can still develop into something, the sun stays always the same, so the blood blends, the new kitchen appliance is not even paid off, the one that whisks it all together, so that the mother, starting all over, gets pregnant again with the working class and delivers it as something different, after she's been busting her back for years, so that she finally will have some peace, because she must give birth. Thousands of rebirths has she been waiting to become something else, for once not a mother!, for once a piece of revolution, please, but the mother has had another miscarriage and gave birth to nothing but a journalist who doesn't know what to say, I don't know either, don't ask me!, I'd say, at the moment it looks rather like the opposite of working class, even though it was so useful for the King to even become king. But that could change and then we'll vanish in the working class or in what's underneath, though they already are the dregs, well, the bottom, and that's what most are already, you too among all others. Your relatives move around, so that they won't be found at home and get hit up for money, that they won't be taken for a fool, that they get paid back, like Oedipus did to himself, why not, but working will be more work for us than writing and the old folks like myself will not be able to participate, because they reached life's last stop, unlike the King, besides, it makes no difference with a king. The King has been accepted by and large, albeit not by all.

Patricide has already brought the greatest fulfillment, I fulfilled mine when I was young, it was fun, what else could I lose now? My smart phone? Couldn't care less, don't own one, don't use one. I am useful to the working class, but I just see it that way, and therefore it hasn't won again this time. It didn't acknowledge me as its mother, fucked it is nonetheless. It dwelled among us and it did not win, though it fancied it would. The majority won, but what? Do you believe that a god is directly involved in this or is it the writers, who wrote it into action and kept it going by tearing it apart and starting all over again and again, so that it won't get finished? Anything but working! Yes, this is my honest opinion.

Well, that's gonna be something. They no longer implore, the workers, who always set out to labor in order to create something, but it is their procreation, and now they are here and so many to boot!, what can you do?, far too many have procreated and what can they undertake now, that is, what will the undertaker, ahem, the entrepreneur whose enterprise is climate control undertake with them now? Not everyone can develop something useful for humankind, we don't need a plague to bring this to light, though that wouldn't be so bad, debts could be equally distributed among the dead. We don't need air-conditioners. The plague, however, could be cured, the ACs are just there and blow us off, I call that progress, others call it that too, this is deadly for an inventor in writing like myself, he must always start all over again. But this I know for sure: Someone has to rule, and it isn't us now, we are not one, we are not even at one. All wrong! We are not king. We are chiefs of the tainted at best, but we are not filthy rich. We are now, we are kings in our house, which, however, we'll soon lose to the bank, we are the supplicants and perhaps must leave, let's hope unscathed, the country, we hope we know someone, be it in another country, who will take us in, for we cannot stay here. We won't get a house again and no foot on the ground. With you at any rate, whom do I mean here?, whoever, we can't stay with you. We cannot be with you, King, we have no place next to you, you have an option, unless you already have the title for this court and that one, for playing golf, or this casino, also for playing. Even as your dear workers, we cannot stay here, you've got your own, God have mercy on them. No problem for him. God says: You just have to put your cross in the right place, I already showed you how that looks, I'll carry it. We are somewhere else anyway, where there is no option. We've always been at home everywhere, that is to say: nowhere. But you, Mr. King, you are at home here and you have your houses of cards here, you are anchored in the bankers, the bastards issued from incest, because we don't deal with strangers unless we want to become king, no, we are anchored in the banks. By the way, it isn't true that the bank always wins, yours does but you first had to inquire, because you don't understand the game that is yours. You don't understand your stakes and what's at stake for us, because we always bet on the wrong thing. You won't meet anything unpleasant, because we'll be gone. Up to now we were more than here, now we're goners more or less.

Hey, you must have a complex regarding this man, regarding any man! Get over it, get with it. Your complex must be dropped, because the time of dissolution has come. You should quickly dissolve your complex, or you'll become unhappy, pregnant with doom as you always are. You are not a savior, you are not one who talks but one who writes, it is quieter, makes less noise, okay, have it your way, there is no one, literally no one who listens, they are listening to someone else. You and your kind are no longer important, go ahead, wait till you are blue in the face, but nothing will happen. You must follow the sister, who will guide you not like a blind king, follow you must, albeit unwillingly. You can talk as much as you like, this time of dissolution will put an end to you, the complex must go now, it's high time, where did you get it, that it lasts so stubbornly, better than your marmalades. Don't bite into the wrecking ball, it makes no sense, the whole complex, this gigantic complex of concrete has to go, in one single quiet move, it's no longer well anchored, it has to fall, like milk teeth fall out, when the definitive ones are moving up. Now they are here. They are here. The teeth still resist, but they must come out. Everything that bothers us about ourselves must come out. The teeth actually wouldn't have bothered us so much except when they hurt.

We are not bothered, not bothered by what?, well, I mean, nothing bothers us, but it bothered so many people, no, they didn't bother, they didn't even notice us after all, but they wanted something else. They did not know what they had, they only knew they wanted something else. So now something from my treasure trove of experience, which should flow some time into a sentence about experience but none is coming to mind yet, nevertheless I would not mind digging into this treasure, it's nothing but debts, those are the debts of indebtedness, of guilt, it's all the same, it never ends, our Father forgive us our debts, it has all been said and in the meantime I have been talking about me much too often, I know, but I don't know anyone else or I would take him, you really want to know what I am striving for now? Being able to pay back my debts to my daddy! But they are so many and daddy only was one, but in this case it is true, no idea what it is, the thing about debts is the only thing that remains forever, it is real, the guilt is real as well, I lived through it, because I brought it about myself.

The little girl who wanted to think of herself as the father's favorite lover, had to experience a hard punishment by her father, she spilled hot tea over the night table that was more valuable than she and more valuable than the father, otherwise he wouldn't have had to hit hard, truth be told, Mr. King, yes you, the heavy hitter who just won the bid, in truth?, and so for the girl the sky is falling. After that she'd played herself up for decades, so that she'll be loved, but she always only accomplished the opposite, she puffed herself up, and now, not even hard punishment, now she has no say in anything, while saying was the only thing that was or should be left of her, that's what it lived for, the child, I mean, without saying anything I wouldn't exist at all, and now I get thrown out, written off even by myself, usually always lifting the writing of others, now my own, an unspeakable humiliation, but what should I do? Now stop it, there you are calling for someone long dead, but if he'd come for real, you'd really be up shit creek! So the princess gets thrown away, the pea shaken out of the bed, it was only one anyway, I disappear together with her. Hold it now, just a moment. Never to fail was up to me and now, and now, and now it's you who never fails, even though I was, of course, destined for it. And now you won. You are my ultimate humiliation, Mr. King, yes, Mrs. King, you too, but you don't count, you count to three, wham, bam, done, then you split, you split to score some more, no, you don't do that anyway. You two get rid of types like me, that's enough, even though they don't even exist for you, you get rid of them, you know you don't like them. As gods, you let me have it, the raging woman, that's all I can do, scream and put on quite a show, men have shown me how to do it, I wasn't good at imitating it, I tried hard, but I couldn't do it. They advised me to hang myself entwined in a woven rope, but I didn't do it, even though it was often suggested to me; they stood around, those men, the King's men, each one a little king himself, or they wouldn't be here, but it was not his fault, it was not his default, such default would have forced them down, but they want to stand up straight with a glass, well, rather sit, right,? in front of their display, in front of the screen which doesn't lie to them, except when numbers come up on it, huh?, so they stood very close to it, but they didn't show me anything, only the no-show of the hoped-for satisfaction, which I could still manage myself even in old age, as a blind seer or, if not, that I could still say something, as a handicapped woman with a cane, which she crash-lands on people, it's her favorite activity, rail at people, blame them, accuse them, stupidly imitate the spazzes, who else will do it?, the King?, no way! Doesn't matter, I often use this term, now it really doesn't matter, I am and it doesn't matter.

The no-show of the hoped-for satisfaction, oh dear, it'll have consequences, though not here, this is not a series when the signal gets lost; everybody can hope for satisfaction just by reaching for the breakfast cereal box. The sense of loss that follows because nothing's inside, is very unpleasant, no loser imagined it like that—it is not pleasant because the body simply has had it and because words are for shit anyway since someone else shits money, and that's holy, at least that's what the King claims and he is full of it. Well, yes, the

Germans are too, especially the Deutsche Bank, the boss of the Germans who always have good intentions to save, but it never works out, they simply own too much, it wouldn't be worth it anyway, this bank lies as well, in the truest sense, whereas the King's speech flushes like the water into his gold toilet, as for himself, his face is always flushed, his cash flows, and also his debts, they get flushed, he will be forgiven just as credits are given to him. No one offers any information let alone reformation. So, now the King has seen his wife who hanged herself, for God's sake, not now!, maybe later, no, it wasn't that long ago, it was just a few lines ago, and it's only been said, cited and re-cited, it could also be several pages, with me, after all, the same is written on every page, and still it is not true, well then: The no-show of the hoped-for satisfaction that anyone would still listen to me, to us *Dichter und Denker*, the poets and tinkers, uhm, thinkers does surprise me. In fact, it was firmly promised to us. But once again only a few were left in the house to watch with schadenfreude, how this satisfaction isn't coming, it always is interrupted like my wireless, when I want to listen to the radio on the tablet, even though the workers in Korea worked so hard and cheap on making it, without knowing, however, what they made, they don't understand their own product anymore, doesn't matter, it often happens to me too, and there are fewer and fewer workers, they don't count, the product will soon produce itself and then it will be our God, who also came to be by Himself and out of Himself, an autocrat—, I mean auto-creator, and if they count anything, the workers, then always the wrong thing.

They should take a look for once, how come that something comes with missing pieces and another with the wrong ones. Botch job. Sometimes it even goes up in flames like the workers who are fired by their work. The device is made in small steps by several workers, none of them overlooks the whole thing, but not even Marx had an overview or only with great effort, and no, since you're asking: You don't get satisfaction from doing something, it only satisfies when you get it without doing something. Do the unemployed even know this? This absence of daily satisfaction which ultimately always leads to conflict, sorry, but it will have terrible consequences, if only for us, the failure of the failed which will happen more and more frequently, it's been long expected anyway, because without fail we'll no longer have anything to say, we haven't in a long time. And we are not used to it, oh humankind! You have to interfere more strongly in what is going on, it is not enough for only your sex to interact, it effects nothing, your life is not nothing or is it?! What does the King say? He says, everyone is worth something, the King just has to still think about how much and who and for whom. Don't say that, you, all of you, don't say anything now, it can be used against you, there is something and it sure is something, yes, we can see that too. You can't even find your feet in the dark, unless you are wearing socks in bed, but there is something foreign about it, which might disturb you! Oh, that makes us sad. Do we really count for nothing?

Another woman who is bleeding
from the mouth for a change:

Nothing at all? Is that really it? We didn't know. Oh no, what must we hear, poor us, it breaks our heart, the ailing country, yes, that too, it tears apart like the curtain in front of a temple and what's beginning here, what's coming into being is no house of cards with cards without faces on them, it is already the new misery joining the old. It was not expected and yet it came, misery, this cruel bond. Oh, please, does it have to be? Yes, it must. Go back to your country or better yet, keep out!, build the wall, no more dough for you, take off your headscarf, now!, or I'll tear it off you! Then your brother will punch me in the face, because he didn't want to be my brother. Obey this prompt or get out! Your parents will be deported now or not be let in and get stuck in an airport! We snatch your food, because you've snatched ours for so long. We barge against you intentionally, that happens more and more frequently now, the stairs fly, no, someone's flying down the stairs, ouch, that must hurt! Who did that now? He's gotta fucking get outta here and back to his country! At least he's got one. Europe's finest! As fine as Tante Fini's famous flour brands. He lucked out by the skin of his teeth. Anything else? Nothing else, because I can't think of anything else.

We have nothing to say, because no one listens to us anymore, and it's better that way, we have no more to say, because it's only us, only us listening to each other, in the book of faces, in the picture book, no, no speaking there and, let's hope not much writing, we can't read any more, we've got problems with it as is. Don't write too much there!, or my own striking but never scoring writing would be superfluous, though I am trying so hard! Yes, all of us are in that book, everyone but me, because I've lost my face long ago; but the others lost even more so; the more faces they won, the less worth is their own face, which betrays their thinking and their fate, even when you look at it only briefly, it disappears among the countless others, even though not all of those like you. They are all lying, they all like you because they want you to like them too, otherwise they won't; be happy: After all, the others also lost. They have all been preserved in your hole of faces until it was full and groaned under the sweet-and-sour marinade, one never knows if one gets praised, but there is always the hope, everyone feels like a winner, because they've got that far and were it only a photo in the book of entrails inspectors, yes, that would be nice, but there's no looking into humans, as much as you might like to. They can roar as horribly as they want, they can untie the rope around the neck, yes, the one around the nation, something got in there, the woman got it in her, whatever it is, is this a pin? Why a pin? It is highly unlikely that someone has a pin sticking in her dress, except for a brooch attached to it, possibly one designed by the daughter, how priceless!, but I still wanted to report how I was beaten by my father, okay I beat him too, but we won't talk about that, others were also beaten, much worse than I, but all that counts for me is what happened to me.

And so, you see, because everyone thinks like that, they now have the King they deserve, he beats them every day and they enjoy it, because they deserved it, they deserve entertainment, since they can't sustain themselves anymore. All they can do is try to contain the pain. Tennis or golf, makes no difference, he beats you, his brand is hotter than ever, he builds towers, he's got one already, more are to follow, he doesn't wax philosophical, he just bangs it all out, banging, no, beating everyone, as I was beaten, when I was also a queen, well, let's say a princess in anticipation of a life which did not come. What says the man? No one else is saying anything. Only the man talks, he has the floor, he is the word, he is the beginning and the end, the Alpha and Omega, the first and the last [thing you'd want], I reversed the [Biblical] order here, for me first still is always the beginning, it still allows hope for a sooth-singer; well, that's what you'd like to be, banging out bogus is more like it. Still, there must be something about him, so let's ask him what he thinks, he thinks: Behold, I come quickly along with my payment to give each one according to his works, and we especially like giving to the workers, because they were the first to loyally stand by us, but they always came last. Now they will be first, but I don't yet know what we'll give them, because we cannot care for them, now that we received the highest honors and are ruling the country, we couldn't care less. They only think they are suffering, they don't even know what suffering is. They don't know what's running down their cheeks. They can't enter our house, that's fully booked, they don't need to read any books for that.

Anyone who loves me follow me or not, whatever he likes, there will be no award for it, but also no rebuke. The economic program will now be imported, the computer doesn't understand it, it can't calculate it. The King says: I just dish, I don't give. What might be new about it: Blessed are those who do my commandments, that they may have right to the trees of life and may enter through the gates of the city and construct their buildings, at any rate those I haven't yet built, and those are not many. Sure thing. So let's wait until the snake bites us in the heel. I think his wife, the King's wife was sneakier, that is why she snuck ahead much faster in the long serpentine line, faster than us, the small-fry lovers, who stopped, who stopped developing, but I should not talk for all women, let alone in connection to daddy, that's just not done; his wife, however is something else, something I am not, sure thing, she is really beautiful, she spent a lot of money on it, on being beautiful, she outstripped everybody, she's made it, she had herself be made over a few times for this, complete make-overs, and now?, and now?, she is ageless, not me, sadly, I am old, I am out of the question, I don't know the answer either, because I didn't hear the question, on top of the blindness there is also the loss of hearing in old age, but also on all the other grounds, where no one wanted to live anymore, even if they were offered for free. Out of the question. Stop building now? Now that I have so many I can bank on? Never!

He himself, who am I talking about here? If I mean you I should say you, but that makes no sense, you would never listen to me and all the others follow your example, we are done talking, we are not finished talking, but we were cut short, the word was cut off in the mouth, first it was turned around and around to see if something could still be swallowed and then cut. We fell silent, the more we talk the quieter we are, we find no counter-love, no counterpart, no contrarian, nothing. We already decided on the reading for the coming weeks, it is your wonderful economic program, which you, however, do not need, we take it, many thanks, but we don't get it. The only good thing is that now we will think about what happened, the thought will drag the deed behind it and then it will meet the deed that won't need a thought anymore. Poor us, will we now have some quiet after the torment, so that we can read up on it all and then take over the leadership again? No way and if, not here. No peace. Don't let your own defeat play you for a fool! Don't let yourself be seduced to respond to a breach of taboo with pleasure? No, taboo breaches are committed with pleasure, we, however, we don't feel like it.

How far and where on earth does one get on this path? The GPS misled us before, that's why we are asking. You there, come here and don't hide, there is a furrow, sow your self into it, help yourself! You are king, mind you, because many are like you, hanging in the waiting line like on a rope, no, not that one, the queen hangs there already, you too might want to become king, figure out how to get rid of your wife then, find out here! The rule of law that no one can be king prevents it. Many are guilty, many more owe us. Forgive us our debts as we forgive others? Out of the question! Debts of flesh are something entirely different, and not everyone wants to have something cut out of him except if it must be done and the doctor stands by with his axe. Did you mean carnal guilt? The partner's right to demand sex—from both sides at that!—was even granted to the woman then, everyone could demand sex from the other and then the other way around. It was called settling debts, it means doing one's duty, the Deutsche Bank reminds us, the most loyal of loyals, the only one that's still getting fucked, that's still waiting for a settlement and therefore also fucks whatever it finds, always someone else, many others, so that the individual won't notice so quickly. It doesn't dare to with the King. It wouldn't do it any good anyway. The only one that still was lending, albeit to a king and still trusting the credit system. Those credits bleed from many wounds which will soon dry up, the bleeding will be stopped; people will also have stopped talking; so many wounds, you see, this is the same with every woman who also has holes from where it is easy to bleed, yes, sadly, there is no difference in this regard, when it comes to blood, she is not different from me, in anything else she is; holes, I ask myself how did they get in there, the holes? What weapon shot them into them? What weapon which some took up, but others did not? Oh, I see, these holes, not all, but many come from this compass needle, that's a totally new use, but then it goes in the wrong direction. Not what you think, not that needle, the holes come from this relatively small pin that offers no safety, just stars and stripes and, since you are asking: The King won't come now, he'll come again tomorrow, but not now, he's talking on TV, how could he be here?, he takes this needle out of his wife's dress, why, it's on TV, oh, it's a tape, he takes the needle from his wife's dress, because his daughter's bracelet won't work as a weapon, it's only expensive, good for nothing otherwise, the King strikes out, it can't be true that he's doing this, but we thought that about him many times, and he does not pierce his own eyes, he isn't crazy to do such a thing, ha, so what does he do with that stupid needle, this can't be true, I just see him actually doing what he intended to, I wouldn't have thought so, I'd have thought he'd still want to see and contemplate his new buildings for a while, no, he reckons, ruling— others shall do it, building, still some others shall do that, they won't do it again, and he does not exclaim, say, this: Never again shall they see, the eyes that is, the horror I suffered nor the one he did—at this point the Deutsche Bank always starts to weep bitterly, because it only hears this Never-Again, that's all it hears from the King, whose eyes are wide open, as if through them he could see something no one else does. But this is exactly what he wants to prevent with the needle, he isn't totally stupid, is he?, if you want to gouge your own eyes out, you should close them before, so you don't see the needle coming, right? If you want to gouge others', you should do it too, then you won't see how small they are. What did I want to say? Okay, what he doesn't like, the King, are preventers, he likes enablers, he, whose eyes will only see the dark he is himself, he calls out unspeakable stuff, because he can't say it, this is why he has to yell it; does he want to expel himself from this country? On the contrary, he finally wants to bring darkness to his eyes and altogether keep you in the dark he longs for. Then he would finally have his peace.

Okay. Without eyes he may stay here, but he can do that anyway and when he leaves he should take his blind eyes with him, his buildings stay, they are real estates, they are immobile, they can only be blown up when no one wants to own them anymore. No, the King does not leave, please, he says, more darkness for me, then I will—all by myself, only I will step into the light and I'll be the only one to be seen, because I'll have shaken off all others, without their ballast I will be able to step out much faster, dart out like a fish into the swarm of countless gnats. It is clear to him now, he shouldn't have looked at this, not strove for what he saw and embraced, the braces drop, he sings his misery, too bad he won, he wished he didn't, all the mischief he could do now and will do anyway, thus singing of ills he drives—I am telling you because you asked earlier, he strikes the pin several times, not just once, though once would have been enough, his wife's jewelry, right, the brooch that gets affixed with this pin, he gave it to her himself, the brooch, designed by the daughter?, no, the daughter didn't design it, not this one, so he struck his eyes again and yet again. And the bleeding eyeballs gushed and stained his beard—no sluggish oozing drops but a black rain and bloody hail poured down. I wish I wrote this. But no god can help me to do it as well or at least half as well. At best he'd chase me through heaven's course, no, curse. Until I'll finally lose my nerve and look for another god. God bless. Well then, now that he has caught his breath, the King—after a long fight in the course of which he sat and ate with his undergods in the golden hall—made himself to see how much he will have to work now, how much more than before, he drinks from his golden cup, he sits on his little golden stool, he sees himself in his golden mirror, he rinses his dental implants in his golden toothbrush cup, no, not those. What's in store for him is horrible, they will pour him nectar and he won't like it, they will give it to him straight, but he won't like that either, he doesn't go for 100 proof, he just likes it hot, he will have to find upbeat as well as upright words which he's swept under the rug before, now they'll drag them out again, oh God, it's all so horrific, not what's behind him, that was terrific, legendary, with the gods and all that, just like it goes in legends and then the King will also enter the world of sagas and fairy tales. Nothing is fact, but everything is true, buy now, maybe later it won't be here anymore, and if you don't want to be it, whatever it may be, then at least buy an apartment in this tower, you won't be able to do that either.

We won't get the honest-to-goodness truth, only the goods, so help me God in here anymore either, and I can't get myself together anymore either from so much rage, which sadly I can't sing, only wreck nerves with and I can no longer arouse lament, I can't arouse anything or anyone. That is the sad truth, which in a sense goes for all of us. What we say is as if never said. What should we do now? Where to start? And then we'll wish we'd never started. We should have said it sooner and to others, when there still was time, that is the sad truth. What we say is as if never said. The King overlooks all this and contacts the Chinese, and then the other Chinese, those on the mainland, he wants to do something with them, which in turn the other Chinese don't like, so much for a good start and it hasn't even started. He is happy because he does not see his *Volk*, he only sees the *Volk* who cheer him, they are not even enough to make a *Volk*; oh God, that is, seen from above a lot of folks whose views he wants to mold, but really doesn't want to, that would be work, he does it all, he doesn't do it, he never did, how should he, what for, why should he have done it, they've all been molded already, everything's been molded and growing mold already!, and then he gouged his eyes out, both of them, he didn't have more or he would have taken them too, so he gouged his eyes out, got it?, he's already got so many thorns in his eyes, he can't see a thing anymore, so he can do without his eyes, he already gouged everyone else, so what else is there? Everyone is at his disposal, but he doesn't want them, he didn't think he'd need them any time, so he threw them out, before he could want them. Now he could use them, all those old sinners of his kind who helped him decisively, among them those who speak with many words, but can't say anything because someone forked their tongues, whoever it may be, he should have stuck to the eyes, they are not needed for giving speeches. Here they all stand, the build-ings, which dread fires and water, both cut to the bone. The ruler does not want this and he does not want to be addressed either, he delivers his own address, he says what he found out earlier and from a god to boot, he only says what he knows. I won't shame, no, I won't bother to name the heroes with their majestic gaze, no, not heroes, I mean Hera, I won't shame her now. All that's left for the King who's got everything, but owns nothing, when it comes to be taxing, I mean taxes, his tax returns—what's left for him to still do, no, no shaving the head yet, no growing a beard, no, and it's not reconciling whatever peoples, who could never stand each other, what could he do about that?, he couldn't have done anything against the Chinese, therefore he is doing something for them, so the only thing left to do: over and over again he must stand by his decision to gouge out his eyes, lest he be blinded by himself to such a degree, that he no longer sees what he actually does not want to see, but prescribe to his people—namely: moderation. He wants to be a role model, but only if it does not involve work. Nation, please never imitate such a gruesome stance, who then would still be a worker, a brand of humans, on whose side we unshakably are, not the King, however, though he calls them men much honored in his country, so that's where we stand until we want to try another brand; who should do all the work if no one sees anything and the worker sees nothing of his work either, he gets nothing out of it, who then should do anything?

The King shows the *Volk* what it should see, to wit him and no one else. I intentionally do not say: nothing. He does not have to see himself, he is, he knows, he knows who he is and there is no one next to him. He will always remember himself, when he no longer sees himself. Now first let's have balls until the balls drop, the women drop first, they are lying there already, how dandy, their holes are predrilled already, they only have to be deepened, very convenient for her as for him. There is no one like him, that's all, why would he still want to see?

There won't be a lack of crowds either, never again, and they won't be reined in either, there will always be lots of people there who want to congregate, we guarantee that much. So then no lack, and no one will reign except one, the healthiest of all, yes, he's the one who rightfully reigns now, the King, he does it better than anyone else. The woman shall not reign, she is not made for it, when it comes to women, the target is never one single head—unless she is a model, a mold for others, which can be filled and poured out; all heads get hit, for woman is the lack everyone suffers from. Enumerated now will be the complete, competent men who also-ran under arms, that's right, they stopped complaining, they lunge out now, I can see it happen with me. I stand between two armies, an awkward position between the fences and the peoples armed to their teeth, and what do I do with them now, if they start moving in my direction? And that means all of them. What do I do with the horse-mastering Trojans who cheerfully mess around in the computers, what do I do with the light-embraced Greeks who couldn't even stand without our braces, who, on their own can only incur debts, that's all they are good at? What do I do with that woman, who testifies against me, who claims something, which can't be true?, it's more likely true what Hera or Pallas Athene or whatever their names are, all those women, then it's more likely true what they are telling the army, so that it lets the enemy smash in their faces instead of having a pleasant chat with him. Though it's not necessarily true either what I am saying about them, they can also be put through the mangle, if they can take it, if so desired, by the steam-heated mangle, for those who like it hot, oh well, women, women, women, how can I put it, she can also be preferred cold, put on ice, the lady, I won't say who, she is the desire, which is also mine, to be a real woman for once, not one who wants to be elected queen, but a real one who'd never want this, she has enough with herself and the children, that's the snag, I don't have any, she has enough to do with herself, as the King does too or her happiness ends or what she took for happiness. Now the woman knows that her erstwhile happiness actually was happiness, but now? Only moaning and confusion, death and humiliation, but we won't go there now, we don't want to take it that far, why bother, she is always very close by anyway, the woman, the goddess, so, actually, every woman, don't turn around, it wasn't for our gratitude she did it, the thrashed one, no, don't trash, save!, the chosen one. One of them surely will let herself be chosen. She will certainly never move far from the viewer, the creator-viewer looking through the viewfinder, throwing focus, she is always there and takes the child to school, this is the unpractical part of this invention, one can either keep something or trash it, I mean thrash it. There is a name for all evils, but what the ruler said about women we drop under the table, they can suck it up later, when they kneel before me, we'll simply drop it, like a word, we ignore it, other stuff is more important, which has been and gets pointed out. I can't give an account here of the stuff that doesn't count, I won't even be done in fifty years and I certainly won't have that much time. No one's missing, but the woman's name is still missing, I don't miss it, but it's missing, because nothing became of her and I didn't manage to get her to be something either. How and as what should she present herself? I would suggest: as grandmother and dog owner. Let's not talk about it. She disappeared and she could never be performed, she is one of a kind, the doctor trashed the cast that was to maintain the form, but it was so moved it melted away. Now the woman is so alone!, maybe it was the wrong material, at least for this project and had to be abandoned, who knows, who?, the King?, even he would no longer pull it off, he can't fit the two sections back together as a regular body, I am not talking about the black Dahlia, anyone who'd ever seen a woman could arrange such parts properly. One goes on top, the other below. It didn't help her to be hot, because she was not even hot, she didn't need to be, she was cold. But if she was supposed to be cold, she would have, incidentally, been hot all over. She should always be as desired thinks the King, who doesn't see it but still finds it good, he finds many good, but he finds only a few who come with him. Forget the woman, the King no longer knows her either. We have to forget her. Only his relatives really love the King, the others despise him but elect him and those who elect him despise him. No, none of this is true, everything concerning woman is not the way it is. This woman can be exchanged any time, well, not the next four years, personally, I believe that four years won't last four years. And old age will cut folks anyway. Who could hold together the herds after them? They can't imagine that, the rulers.

It did not even splat, water doesn't do this all the time, it has to recover again in-between and smoothen its surface with even more superficiality, splat! And gone it was, the entire surface, the expensive incisions pulling the eyes upward, the varnish that's supposed to cover it, the injections supposed to keep it in that condition. What's happening here with her?, now I am talking about the other, the real wife who wants nothing but the King. This one wants this, the other one that, this one wants it all, he even puts up with lack, if it's the right kind, with me it's the lack of ideas, which is my problem not yours, you, after all, are free to leave the room anytime, I can't do this and usually, if one has no more new ideas, there always are old ideologies and other countries to bomb, but that's not what's coming to the King's mind either, well, let's hope so, he only minds bombing on TV and keeps his mind on other, new buildings, in which and with which to rip off others. Not water, which is already here. What can you do? Spring from a rock and welcome the chosen in a chosen place, before the asocial media who don't say what they want, only whom or what they don't want, get wind of it. How about it? Something else for a change. Then I'll blow into this small tube. It's still a far cry from a wind. So, what can you do? What are you waiting for? Nothing, those folks have everything already, they've had it. Horns are already crowning the heads, I wonder why, watch out, the bulls will shortly return from the bull market, human hordes, swimming atop the foam of their own rage, because the bear is loose, are trying to provoke them so that they would win after all, the bulls! They poke and kick them. Full cover!

Now storming at him in packs, like herds of cattle, are the men who want to finally get to be something too. After their acts of violence, they vanished unnoticed, now they are back again. In the meantime, they've been around in the world. Hands reached out for theirs, they were implored, for a bit more pay or a bit more death, as the case may be. But they had nothing to distribute. They were sent off, sent to the field, the pasture of death-bound livestock. They are coming from places, many places they had visited themselves whose cities should, whenever possible, no longer be recognizable, hotbeds of misery, ruins shall be the fate of these places. What?, that's supposed to be a city? Now we really can't believe that. People don't like dying in traffic, they'd rather die in wars. Let them go, for this is the highest honor we've got, say the gentlemen with the stars, not the stars in the sky, but on the shoulders. Do we send them away or let them stay here?, what, the stars?, no, not those, say the gentlemen. Or do we quickly open a fast-food chain or do we close it again? This chain, however, you too can have, the King's daughter designed it herself and wrapped it around herself, look, isn't it pretty, and you can purchase it! Exclusive!, which means only you can buy it and bring your relatives and friends, they may want to buy it too, this kind of chain, it's not a fetter for you, quite the opposite. It's others who will be fettered. Or do we eat it all up, here you go, take a plate? Such beautiful jewelry! Those beautiful clothes, shoes, bracelets, the entire collection! Vanished! Simply gone. Such unfair treatment. This chain necklace is not even available in this chain anymore. Kindly, buy it where everything is available. Buy ether, no buy in the ether. Such a good person, the daughter, treated so meanly, so unfairly! Please keep buying all the more now. So terrible. Treated so badly. All unfair. Please buy elsewhere now. Be fair and buy elsewhere, but the same! Buy elsewhere, absolutely, keep buying, but no need to be fair.

So, those men were abroad, like us, not like me, the military are always abroad, there isn't much to do here. Here the men learn to go to foreign countries and behave. Foreign countries, where I haven't been very often, those men know them, it was their mission to commit dark things, dreadful stuff and communicate them afterwards. They know foreign lands, the most powerful of the citizens there crawled in the sand around them eating crow. Was this even worth all that zeal? Was it worth being able to later reign and react? The men, hit hard, are holding back for now. That's required at the moment. They do what is requested. They know the chain of command and wait for their turn to bring peace; peace they yell, we aren't doves, we are hawks, I mean, don't yell like that, we aren't deaf! Yes, you know it too, this burger chain, they've got one, they are forming a line now, the Burghers, a chain for peace. Doesn't matter, we did that too, way back and what good did it do? None. By your stars we shall know you, General, Sir. The one who has three or four stars on his shoulders gives more orders than he receives. You bet. Do you have any idea what it means to get that far? I have no idea, I haven't been anywhere yet, I am quietly following my path, I am on my way, I am not a general, I don't travel abroad—as often admitted to and certified—but in anger I hit anyone who wants to eliminate me and he actually hits back! Well, he'll pay for it the same way, I don't need a general for that. Now the man of the center plummets from the midst of us and no matter where he falls, I'll kill them all, I still have to catch them though. We won't need generals, they are all here now, nothing to be done about that, but I wouldn't let them into my home. Citizens will no longer build houses, they now have generals to build them up—men who do not want to be addressed, in any event not by some citizens whom they don't know. Generals are important. They kill but they do not defile the beds of the dead. So, now we have done it, now everyone's running, no, not the generals, of course, they signed a contract that they will never run away, unlike the King who unfortunately is liable for millions of people, the generals are never personally liable. That's a great life altogether, exempt from personal liability and from getting locked up, don't you think so? If as a refugee, one can never see one's loved ones again, never enter the homeland which the generals wrecked, nothing but ruins there, then we'd rather go somewhere else, right?, and nothing, nothing, nothing would help, it would not help us either to kill the one who begot and raised us. If he is still within reach. The generals would get him anyway, no, they wouldn't, they'd ruin anything and everything and always all of it, even that which they don't get. And that's something we wanted to take on ourselves. But not now. Maybe tomorrow again, but not today. They know how it is when something breaks, no matter what, and they don't do that anymore, the generals. They let it be done. They know the ropes, no matter where. Everywhere. They have the right word for everyone and the right deed. They've always been somewhere else, from our point of view, we know why, they've always been in places that rocked. And whatever didn't rock, they wrecked with their rockets, they even made walls dissolve in dust, they rocked alright, and then they knew the way the cookie crumbles. Better to get away alive from those mortals than dying themselves. And that means, fast enough, before they are met by a disaster they'd brought themselves, but don't want to take back home again, they don't want to have the war back home. Chain of command there, chain of command here, where we don't accept any commands though, we just give them, we've got everything, we give nothing except commands and what goes on there, where we give commands? No grass will grow there anymore. It is also quite important to not just move around as a simple wanderer who wants to see a bit of green. One has to move around as a general, every king needs one or more of them, ideally more, they tell the

King, we don't just move, we run. We are world shakers. Wherever we show up, the world runs away from us. It doesn't do it any good. The herds also run wherever they want, this way and that, and now there finally are men who give them the lowdown, they can already smell the slaughter-house, the herds, let's go there! On the count of three. Oh, it's a no go after all? No slaughter? Let them slaughter their animals themselves, if they want to see blood? Okay, fine with me too.

The men with the stars are peaceful now, that's why they were brought in, to be peaceful, which they could have been anywhere, but such restraint was not desired before. In general, this kind of strain isn't good. It's against their nature, though it's not more than their nature either, which is against itself. Writing something in the sand first and then wiping it out. Wiping out is less work. Even I am peaceful, that's no big deal. I don't need men for that, those men on top, yes, indeed, on top, yesterday still elsewhere, but also on top. Death made them cautious. But they don't bring death now. They did once and now the shaker is empty. That's progress for the men of the Nothing. They brought it, now they are giving us nothing. Why would they. It's already here. They brought us the Nothing, now they take it back again. That costs a pretty penny but, mind you, it's for a good cause. Everything costs. So then they've seen the Nothing, the men, surely something, no one can be expected to go through anymore. It used to be. So hup hup, take the dive, head first, into the Nothing, it's so inviting, also for us!

Just a moment, no, as of right now that's over with! Back to the beginning, which isn't one! Never again nothing. We know it, we don't want it anymore. We've got in over our head in debt, now we keep still. Pardon me, you seem to know the ropes, you've been foisted on us alright, now take the lead, we need a lead, more than a thousand lawyers didn't show us any, now the generals are supposed to do it? Those guys will show us how it doesn't work, after they've always shown us how it doesn't work either, but nothing that did. Never will. They are five, no, four altogether, the fifth owns an entire chain of meat, but doesn't want to pay either. With immediate effect, the generals are the attendants of the man in the royal box. From there they spit down on us, right out of the royal idiot box. Enmeshed they are in a horrendous curse, that now shall get unwired. So here we are, all of us are enmeshed in one fate and don't know it. Only if we pull on it really hard do we notice someone hanging on us, one or more. You don't know what fate you get yourself pulled into, possibly a foreign one, as before? No, let's hope not. We've got enough to do with our own. I dread the premonition that seers will get to be able to see and what will they see? That, which they never wanted to see again, though they don't see anyway. Eternal peace? They would have to show it to us more clearly. What should we show them in turn, what do they want? Peace, made by generals? No worries, they do that on their own. If they can make war, why not peace? It's simpler, doesn't cost a lot, sure. There they come, the four men, with them a herald, who is blowing his horn, no, banging the keys, twitter, twatter, and off we go!

Only generals can initiate peace, they know who and what war is. I don't know it and I never got far with premonitions. That's something for women. Oh, right, I am one. Gotta live with it. At least we'll no longer think of sacking foreign countries. That's good. I vote for that, but can't find the form, I'll mail it to you later. We don't have to go there anymore, wherever it may be. Those foreign countries that matter—been there, done that. We know them all. They are no longer foreign, those we moved into before. We hand it all over swept-clean. Generals think about it, then they do it or don't do it. Or they countermand it again. Can you tell me please, how I get to the top of this chain of command, I'd like to see for once what it's like there, someone new is supposed to sit there now, his name has been announced and blessed and given the blessing. Woe to us, his deeds are already quite transparent, though not his intentions, can't see those. Maybe there is nothing there and the debts tear up holes, which must also be filled again, it must be done. Even if just one creditor requests execution, instant execution, we'll just have to get our generals we no longer need elsewhere, at least not for personal needs. Maybe others will follow suit, oh! Some suites are still available, so sue, ahem, suit yourself. This deal must get the blessing of—I know which commission, but I won't tell. Time for a break, please. Now we will rehearse the answer to the next question. The word insolvency must never be uttered by anyone. The word victory has often been uttered, except there never was one.

Done. Excuse me, how do I get to the legal chaos? No worries. All roads are leading there, just chose one, the lawyer, however, is your expense. Trust the King, who has trusted lawyers for quite some time, he carefully scrutinized them all. Research history and try to find somebody you could trust more! You won't find one. So now the hard drive crashed! But don't worry: the King will also throw something down to you. There is so much he doesn't have, and even more he's already spread in various dumpsters. He can dump his debts there too, while he's at it, he is king now. You wouldn't have thought that this one would want to be that of all things, the way he always vilified the previous king! But let no one be counted as happy ere he has reached his goal, which does not have to be the end of life, not necessarily, say the generals, who'll drop dead off the chair any moment, they are so old, the end can also be somewhere else completely and until then the King will suffer much misfortune, which he will pass on to his customers at the wholesale price. The King touches our hand, a gripping gesture, really. Antibiotics would do a better job. It ought to be antibiotics! Oh, dearest brothers, why don't you sign up voluntarily, right now I don't know why, for what, but whoever signs up will not be taken, because already beforehand he will not be this person's cup of tea, and that one's neither, because he doesn't suit the daughter, because he doesn't suit the son-in-law and that relative will become very important. We are waiting anxiously for it.

Yes, speaks the King, he says much that is true, he tells the truth, the sayer of sooth, but it is wrong. Does he at least take a rest now after the torment? No, no rest, he is restless, so he can't give rest either. He screams the bars should be opened and the country informed that he is a multiple liar and murderer and adulterer, however, not an invader or exploiter, especially not the latter, the other king does that. Will do. Well, okay, so he screams out heinous, unspeakable things, as if he wanted to expel himself, since he happened to become king, he doesn't want that though, never did, he wanted to buy a new hotel, but if he weren't king, he would not get the capital for it and he wouldn't get the occupants for this either, and when all that won't work out, he'll have to build that stupid wall instead, as he promised, no god will help him there, he must, poor him, he cursed his own house and with his own curse to boot, which he must carry out, blind as he is from now on. That's all he needed now! Everyone wished he never knew him. Others wished they always knew him. Too late for that. We needed this one like a hole in the head or like two holes which had been eyes before, oh dear. Or like the holes of a woman, who could wash you away with her blood if you thoughtlessly open the door, the tide is turning, but the woman gets nothing out of it, she puts out, but never lets you out again, except if it pays. That's how they are, we tried it, well, not personally, that is. Not that he would have to account for it, our King, you can count on him, so count yourself lucky and strip, so now he sees the flesh, here it is, prime New York strip, somewhat past it, I'd say, no tenderloin, so the flesh was there, today

this one, tomorrow another, already lying there well prepared and nicely chilled, because this time he wants to play
it cool. The woman should pay no attention to him, he will
pay enough to her.

He didn't put his eyes there, into the fridge, he doesn't need
them anymore, so why ice them? It also works without
them, everything works with him and especially without.
He wants to be king rather than doing kingly business, why
should he, he doesn't have to do anything, he skips the
doing, he just wants to be, he just wants to be nice and
comfy inside himself, and now he receives without fear, well
now, who, whom does he receive?, whomever he wants,
duh! Another prospect, soon to turn suspect. Only the like-
minded, but mind it ain't. The mind hid under the matter,
which will soon blow up, the King will have given the order,
and it shows up again, the mind, not the King, he is gone
most of the time, depending on where the golf course happens to be. He receives everyone he loves as long as he likes
it, then he'll be dismissed. That one there he won't receive,
no chance. If he figures out in time how to get rid of people
so that they go home in tears, he will be happy to show them
the way as he is showing it to millions of others as well. He
is King, after all, on account of a clever process of elimina-
tion. Now there is no one except him. He is the way, he
became the crossroads, whoever wants to follow him, go
ahead, for all I care.

There it is, the nocturnal seed, which he finally wants to look at by day, now brought to light, none of them bringing about anything, the seed brings forth itself, but nothing will come up, a pile of seed, what will it bring in, I mean, who will bring it in? No, whom will it bring something? Could this be the time to bring charges against you, King, if so, will you please tell us? Or do you want to be charged another time? No worries, no one will do it anyway. Maybe I should wait a bit, since everyone does it, file complaints against you, well, if they are many, he is even less afraid, the King. Where others only complain, I would like to contrast favorably, even though I am also complaining all the time.

A horde of young white men say that they are just talking about it, what about?, I don't understand, whatever, now they are the first ones talking anyway, they always are the first to take the floor: Listen, say those who would never listen. Today they intentionally are not talking about what everybody else is talking about, because they think this is the value of *Eigensinn*, own-mindedness that is, that cuts itself off from reason and once own-mindedness is talking, it's only about self-*enownment*, don't you find that odd? Heidegger doesn't. No, absolutely not. They can't be thinking clearly, they do think clearly, they are listened to, they have our undivided attention, the young white man has taken the stage and unlike the poets he does not teach suffering, neither does he need a seer, who envisions it for him, even though he can hardly see anything, because he's got this pointed white hood over his head!, he makes a prophecy, he says what everyone is saying, no, one can't put it that way, he would have to think of something, he says what everyone says without thinking, he says a lot more people will simply disappear through violence. Whatever he can contribute to it, he will do. The seers might as well shut up and go practice until they see something different. The white man answers, but he didn't understand the question, he does not want any more regulation of speech, he makes the rules now, which are, as stated, not regulations but just maybe even law. He is the forgotten working class, he can see that the elites are also at a loss, this is his hour, now he will control the land and sell the voiceless a lottery vote, to each his own lot, no, he will find the ditched ones and hitch them to the masses again and he will give a voice to the masses, unfortunately only one, one voice-one single vote for the ditched masses. Now the tennis ball is descending, the masses cheer, they are getting hitched and pulled along. Now the new time is hiking right along with them. Still, they are only vans, I mean, fans, who crash their vans into the abandoned houses, but those will be torn down anyway, the banks have other things in mind for them, though they don't tell us what, or somebody might want to have his house back. If the ditched get unhitched, they must be given a voice to vote, okay, here you have your voice, half a kilo voice, will this be all? It will be all. They voice one vote. Should we count this one vote one more time, no, I'll count it for you, same difference, one piece of vote, period, and it won't get more either. Everyone got only the one, they speak with one voice. Take the power and shove it up your ass, no, you say it funnier, but I can't do it now, the only one who can do it is the one executing his power, he has risen above it all, what should we do with power? Give it a try and we'll see what happens? Well, let me suggest a compromise: We grab the power and shamefully push foreigners out into foreign lands! Wouldn't that be something? It has to go like that: We are pushing those who are foreigners for us now, but haven't always been, at least that's what they thought, back into foreign lands where they belong now and forever. With forever I mean a time which will last beyond my death, which many will cling to even after my death, because it belongs to them, it was promised to them and they took it. Sadly, for me this forever will be current for a short time only, and the currency will no longer be money, but something else. Ole King Cole was a merry old soul but hateful and angry too.

I accuse you of the sole authorship in this crisis and I am afraid you will also participate in the destruction of the cultural order, oh, you already registered for the course, I see, the course is about to start, where will it lead us? Into those holes I am talking about, but the King does even more, please forgive me, but I am one of the few, who know where they are, as I am a member of a very big minority which, in many circles is called the majority. You have been there and frequently so and, if you wish, go back there once again, become minority, then you can fall, if not on the field of honor, and your wishes will, who knows—I no longer say sublimated— for such words have become superfluous, who knows them still?, nobody, only the upper crust, so, yes, most others just know other words. The Nothing is your mission, Mr. King, I know that this is not your name, it's just the way you are. Now those who desire you so much are calling for you to come out, why not, I say, the others don't, but they are here nonetheless and they shout (note: they do NOT shoot) with those signs, on the street, and that gets protected to boot!, they've been incited by some sort of messengers, they must have been incited or they would not be so excited, why not, I say, what misery are we still missing? As a seer I still have to practice, I can see that, I search for them all, the living and the dead, the dead are easier to find, it is known where they stay. I can't think of any, no misery we haven't had. Perish dishonored, maybe? No, not that. Not being allowed to look at the darling children and the dear son-in-law? No, there is no danger of that. Having to buy the jewelry collection of the wife, so that she won't feel hurt? But she ate it all up earlier, there's even a photo of it! Maybe not necessary. It'll surely sell like hot cakes now. Yes, of course the wife comes along, what?, she isn't coming?, not right now?, advisors, don't advise me anymore! Why are you always saying the wrong thing? How come you say the wife's coming along, when she actually isn't? How come the wife says she is coming, when she doesn't? Okay, not every woman comes with anybody, but this one does, to wit with me, who is everybody. How else could she fill her days of life way over the top? Give an account! Everybody does as he likes anyway. What is there still left for him to love, what to catch sight of? No more, since he's surrounded by all of it all the time? The son-in-law takes notes, the daughter bends over him, she makes a corrective intervention, the father relied on a wrong bill, now he has to come up with a draft of a new bill, lest the crumbs of the old one, which he already finished spill on his pants. This bill won't gain him anything either, because as of now it is he who fits the bill, so why does he do it? No, he doesn't do it at all, he is not entitled to it. He says this is an order: Read up on who is qualified for it. In principle, it really makes no difference, as long as it is a go, as long as anything goes, all going off and away together with the bill, all of reality going off, like a bombshell, like his very self, and disappearing like the people who produce it. What's written here? Over time we recognize it clearly: Time alone reveals a man as just, it takes one day to recognize the bad one. And you want to forbid me to call the King bad? When even Sophocles permits me. Who do you think you are? The angry white man? So go to the Forum or whatever the marketplace is called in Greek and say who, according to you, must be the first to fall and who the next, and who in general and who must fall with all the others and that the rest must fall as well, all of them, except you. So then say it, go ahead, say it!

The King listens to everything and then he reports what he was told. He also asks the augurs for their advice, but they can't read his handwriting and they are repulsed by the stinking entrails that are spread before them. And he really isn't good at writing, the King, he rather does other things with his hands. The workers love him for that. Thank you very much. Oh, please, it goes without saying, you don't have to thank me for being allowed to come, and you don't either that you may stay. I've been allowed to come too, after all, up to now, now no more for quite some time. Not necessary, I am here anyway. If only I won't be made to disappear through violence! I'd like to stay, but just as you wish. You don't yet have to look for me in the land of the dead, whoever you are.

Perfect! We still can get the sight of your wife in here, just in time, onto this sheet of paper, glossy paper, high resolution, well, rather dissolution, no, not that, highly dissolvable, spectral, I mean spectacular, dazzling to the point of blinding, is how she is printed here and can't get away anymore. She can let herself get carried away by talking, but no longer can she get away. She did not find the way. It is not what she sees that counts but as what she is seen, what can be seen is all she is, as she is only a sight to be seen, she is what she presents: a sight, for she is always young and forever, and she better says nothing, she says nothing better, she says what another woman said before her, she does not say more, the other one has said enough, that's enough for three goddesses plus a piece of fruit. Which one will be chosen?, the one who is beautiful, we will win her back by way of a war, like oil out of a rock, millions will die, the rest will drown or suffocate, but for this beautiful woman it will have been worth it in the end and also before. Maybe she has more to say, maybe she actually has something to say, we haven't yet heard anything from her that's not been said already by the other one before her, I don't even understand that much and she does not say it anymore either, she is not yet prepared for the loss of esteemed body parts, because in the meantime her valued body parts have been undergoing ongoing improvements, no, nothing is going under, they are just getting under the knife, so that she can always stay the same, I am sorry, I still don't know her. Well, then open a new page in your computer, just a few clicks, there's a clack and there she is. In order to stay the way she is, she must be changed like all of society, who are here banging their silver knives and forks and spoons on the table, which they already had in their mouths when they were born. Though I was born a long time ago, I haven't changed since then, what comes out of me is always the same, I know the suffering is unbearably huge, albeit not mine, but I can't enunciate it, no, nor sing it, I am becoming more and more from day to day, all around, that is, outwardly, even though my thread of life is getting shorter and shorter, I am already glad if no one cuts it off, at least not before it's been sewn up, lest someone undoes the words I stitched together, beg your pardon?, no, I'm not running anymore, I only run out of time, I have an expiration date while the young white man, the new master of the worlds, where he doesn't have to introduce himself, he, he has ruled for quite some time already, so while he's starting only now, really revving up, I hear a roar, a howl, I am getting drowned out, help!, what did I want to say, I am continuously changed by time beyond recognition, who am I? Who's interested? I can't see my genital region, no, not true, I could take my father's shaving mirror again, which is still in my possession which has come in handy several times, which held up much longer than my old man, and I can leisurely look at it, this region, but I don't want to, I deny it, I deny everything, something's collapsing, is it the word now too, which I seized, or is it a stranger's coat, whereunder, sadly, I'd still be recognized?, no, it is the former, in person! it is the dear, carefully groomed word which I worked on with the word file I made out of my nail file, tinkered, fooled around with until no one wanted it anymore. We are done wording, all of us, we won't get an answer, we, who are like me, listen everybody, we are done talking, for a while we were the talk of the town and, indeed, desired, we even led the public opinion, until it lost its way, but now it's not us anymore, we aren't we anymore, maybe you are, not me, not anymore. Now desire must be redirected to those who are really truly desirable, beyond words, like this woman here, desired, that's all she needs, heard, that's all we need, we don't have words for it either and we don't even know the 'for it.' And no one knows us anymore.

Words are used up and now the upset rule, the ones who were left and now remain as the only ones left. Oh, pain! Now we probably have to hear them every day and they'll get louder and louder, because they don't get what we promised them. They've set themselves up against us for so many years, the disappointed, and now it finally got them something, a sobering up, because they've all been set up. You should feel lucky. You can come here to sneer and leave in misery. Poor you, not even Santa Claus brings you anything. And even the sandman shuts his eyes in agony. Better to be really blind from pouring the sand mistakenly into one's own eyes.

So, is this supposed to be an action? No, it can't be. But something should be happening, no matter what, no matter how, and so with me, as usual, it's always only talk. A children's choir enters, lots of shuffling and whispering, sing, oh you little snacks for gods!, don't wiggle like that, start singing instead, tell me what you want, sing it, oh, you little pains so I won't hear you whisper which is quite irritating for someone musical. Did you poison the social climate? No, you did not, I can see that just looking at you. Are you young voters? Not yet, but soon! What? You are, after all! I knew it! You are singing now: This was an important message, very important, especially for the impoverished inner cities! All of them, mayor, police, radio stations, hot dog vendors, Face Books which are setting the tone, all of them fail to restore order there. Let's hope the King will pull it off. Yes, we very much hope so, he must include the people in the process and against the rest he himself will have to start legal proceedings. Millions of people voted who weren't supposed to. An important, but difficult task, no idea which one, let's sing, oh horror of darkness enfolding, resistless, unspeakable visitant sped by an ill wind in haste, we better go inside lest we get stung by the barbs of giant hornets and wasps, lest we must remember any misery when we grow up. The King must bring all the voters together again, big job, big job, and an important message it is as well. He can be this unifying power, we strongly believe in it. Sure, there were protests, but we, the kids, we the kids, cheerio, tralala, riots too, purumpumpumpum, yes, those too, from the other side, protests and riots, but the King will unify the country. If they don't accept the results, then what, huh? Well, this is why I voted for our King. I hate correctness. Correctness is what we hate most. And we are the most! We are singing, we are singing. Of course it can happen that he too will fail. We never thought he is the savior of the world, so when he makes mistakes, we'll criticize him, yupdidoo, twitter, twitter! Will do! We already criticize him for mistakes he made, you think we don't dare to? Kovfefe! For example, the King has plans, he's got these and then he's got those, on and on and on, one plan after the other. There was another comment about the King, it was pathetic, the women's charges were pathetic, but what do you think, how often we have already heard that in our lives? All the time! Everyone says what he says. Everyone assaults the one he's always assaulted. Everyone assaults everyone except if he knows him. And even then. But we trust him and his daughter is also a strong advocate for him, it's her vocation. She vowed to it and keeps wowing us with her vow: "I am for it." Yes, she defended the King, therefore it cannot be true. No, she would have defended him, had she thought it was true, that is, if the false stuff he said was true. The daughter defended him and this is why I believe her. Yodiyodiyodieyodiyeah. If he does that, if he did something he did not promise us, we will protest. This is the beauty of democracy, twitter, twatter, we must still have it somewhere!, seek, seek, sob!, that's what's so great, twitter, twatter, chirp, chirp, beep, that anyone who wants to can protest. No nasty stuff or we'll criticize, caw caw! We are all of one tree and we shake ourselves but we don't yield anything, we don't give a fig, fuck those nags, twitterditwee, twitterditwee, and another tweet, and yet another tweet and another and one more image to go with it and there the other image, I could go on with this a lot longer!, I am totally thrilled he's our King now, it's a blast! I was so excited during election night!, me too!, me too!, me too!, me too!, tirili, tirila, so excited! We stayed awake until the official announcement of the coming of the Lord, we, the shepherds, all of us, tralala, we, the shepherds, not of *Being*, not of pigs, just shepherds in general, now he just has to implement it politically, now he must not implement anything that endangers groups or he'll be removed from office, we have the opportunity, every four years the opportunity, awesome!, tweet-tweet-twat-twat, or something like that. The opportunity is what's so magnificent about our system. The other one we don't like, we don't like her. We only like the opportunity. Three missed calls and fifteen texts on the smartphone and all of them say the same thing, they are so thrilled and happy, ladiladiladila, they say that now our country will get better, will get better, will get better, let's hope we can all work together and make the country again into what it was, when we didn't yet know it. Happy, Happy, Joy, Joy!, tirili tirili tirili tandaradei tandaradei chitter! He didn't speak well of women, outrage, comments, outrage, comments, like, don't like. Into darkness we look, like he who no longer has eyes, he sings, we sing, the King sings, we sing with him in chorus while he pierces, no, not us, himself!, he is so magnificent, it is not us he pierces, we might not even bleed, he pierces himself, blood runs out of the sockets from where his eyes crawled out, yes, it's also running out of women somehow, but for now just out of him, that's where it's more likely to be needed, he takes away the sins of the world, he redeems us and the bleeding eye-balls gushed and stained his beard—no sluggish oozing drops but a black rain and bloody hail poured down from where he once at least could see us, then his eyes no longer wanted to. They did not want to see us anymore. We all exit singing now, and if with new courage our hearts are filled we can enter again. Off with the choir before it's too late and something else comes to my mind.

Just because you're asking, I have to take every question I can get now, soon no one will ask, let's use the time before it overuses or abuses us: I noticed long ago that I haven't got a dick at an age for which it was provided and now I won't get one anymore either, still better than not getting it up any-more; yet I am not even a god-like being, no, I most certainly am not resembling God, I've seen pictures, I saw his most recent photos, where he looks quite different, still: No com-parison! I did come out of the same crack, no, not the same like this woman who does not speak but is still there, because she got her breaks without one crack in the glass ceiling, I am just a crackpot, that's all the household effects and causes I can and want to and will ever handle, no, sorry, here I see two deep and two flat plates, similar to my writing and there a middling and there another, smaller pot, that's enough for me as just one single person, I have to eat with what I am, bigmouthed somehow, don't you think so too?, I'm still talking, yes, but I am on my way out, I am on my way pushing 80, I'll exit in a moment, there is the door, I can see it, no danger of me running against it. Don't advise me anymore, it's no use. I don't know how I would see my father in the Netherworld, I hope I'll never get there, never!, but if I do, I'd never want to be buried there with my father, because mother also lies there, with her? Never! Now that it is too late, I could look her in the eyes, but I don't even see her eyes, they are gone. All this meant only for my eyes, all done just for my eyes, all those crimes done just for me? Too much honor! No, never again for my eyes! No, just a moment, meanwhile the loss has become imaginable for me, every loss, I've already lost almost everything, and the threat to remove me, to remove me from the stage, to remove me from life— please, no confusing one with the other, is on the table, while others increasingly let lose, they won, after all, this must be celebrated! I will be removed from this table, from this space, because whoever can't let lose must get lost. Let lose with us! You don't really want to disappear, do you? In hindsight I fully realize my loss, which probably has always been there, I've lost myself, for the longest time, but no one looked for me, who should have? No one. How much would I like to let myself be loved by my father, it would have made mother superfluous, but she has been removed anyway, the same way as my father, long ago. What applies to those like me? Who always suffer genital rebuffs for their genius which they don't even have? And for whom then could it have been intended? No one in particular. My masculinity complex opens many doors for me, but not this one. What desire drives me to implore you here like this? Why am I doing this anyway?, no one's talking about me, okay, but sometimes I must be the one talking, since no one else does it, it must be me who's talking. Everyone's talking about the new king, who talks about me? I! And only I! Quickly throw me out of the country, to where I cannot be addressed by anyone! It's just a bummer, that I won't be able to address anyone anymore either.

Oh, someone must have locked up everything in the meantime, I have no other explanation and I don't even know what it is I can't explain. Are you expecting me to flee from this country? Since so many must flee, this path was not meant for me, I thought I would be walking all by myself. Why then are there so many people right here, of all places, where I am? What are they telling me? How I should fit in with them? Could it be that once I had an organ like you? An organ that works really hard, unlike us. Better to find out where we stand in need, where, if need be we could build three steel mills, so that modern power can be produced, or do we need to produce power so that we can have steel mills? I don't know yet either. So then, chop, chop, put your graves in order!, whoever hasn't ordered any should do it now, he should make a deposit like this king, but never pick up the order. Yes, we also accept collective orders for the time when war will be upon us again. I don't think there will be one with Pakistan. Darn it, we'll lose the deposit. He won't care, the main thing is he won't have to pay the rest. Steel and iron break, but not our promise. We get no factories, no steel works, no coal mines, no, really now, not those? They are killing people! We won't have any of that. The King is not a living resident of this city, what for does he need a power plant?, he is himself a power house. Well then! Let fate take its course wherever it goes, I say, let it go. I have no fate anyway, at least none that's still able to walk, thank you, I am fine, under the given circumstances, but I could be better. I could be a man but I am not.

Okay. Let's keep it short, no, not short for sure, no need to thank me that you are getting so much, it's nonsense anyway: Herewith I accept the fact—just a moment, the notary public will be here in a sec—that I am not a man, that I am specifically not this man, not king and not much otherwise, I declare under oath, my dear friend, that I am too small, what?, I should drop dead, will I finally shut up?, yes, soon, I'd like to be a man like every woman except the one, who doesn't want to be, it could even be quite a simple man, I hope he is still available young and white, no one takes the other colors, those are shelf-warmers, that's all they can do. No answers will be given or taken, no, truth to tell, only you answer, albeit not the truth. Only you can be heard answering. What others say cannot be heard, oh well, you don't care, but I do, as a woman I exist for you just as little as I'd exist as a man. I accept it, what else can I do. Where is my place, the one assigned to me, there would be a spot, but the crowd does not part for me, the sea would do it but not this screaming crowd. I am lost and I never find anything, at least not what I need, at the moment not even a pen which I could really use and not for gorging my eyes out, only a man could think of that. Hey, old hag, look here now and tell me what I am asking you! What? You want to tell me you were a slave, you of all people, the way you look? And you, there, what are you doing here? Looking for a job? There is none. Maybe further down. What do you want? Doing what kind of work?, to whom were you assigned, kindly complete this questionnaire! Then we'll get to the psychological part. Yes, you are right, the boy, no, the King, it is the King himself and he fears absolutely nothing, where?, where do you see him?, he is not with us, he is afraid of the execution?, you must be mistaken. He is just extending the suspense?, and with what does he poke himself, his poker hand trumps all the time, where's that poker going, not in the eyes, no and he doesn't cut anything off himself either, it's been cut already. Don't you remember? Well, if I could remember, nothing would have had to be cut off of me.

Somehow it seems to me as if everyone practiced on my thread of life. I know, I shouldn't say that, pure self-pity, especially disgusting, now I shouldn't say anything at all, even though I said it in the past, certainly too many times. Now that we have a king again we should finally be quiet, it can't be changed. But for me this is a general question; How do I say it? That's all I am concerned about. The King already knows. He was the first to be informed and he is also the first to say what he has to say. Now everyone says it, he became father where he himself has, no, not sowed, was sown. The folks who sowed, no reaped, no, elected him, will soon find out about the sacrificial cult, albeit not from me. Just as Abraham had to learn the lesson about the son, what did God tell him? What did he have to say to him. We'll both return from the mountain. So then God would have never requested from Abraham that he sacrifice his dear son. And this is exactly—I think, I've got it now—this is exactly how these factories, these smelting furnaces or however steel is produced nowadays and, most of all, where?, so these factories have all been moved before they had to be slaughtered and gutted. Well, you won't find any more here. Look for them elsewhere, best on another continent. With much water in-between.

The son would have never been sacrificed, God knows it, but do you know it too?, and the factories won't be either and this is because they've been promised by the King plus the work that was supposed to be done in them, but they won't be kept. Those folks came to the King, their own lives tucked under the arm, to supplicate, please!, diligence and industry!, please new mills and holes in the ground and those have been promised to them, just as Jehovah promised Abraham the sacrifice of his son not directly, but required it from him.

So Abraham takes the wood and puts it on his son Isaac, the wood on the son, so he would burn better, sure, some fire under his ass, no, under the smelting furnace, which no longer exists, and if it does, then in India or China, that's too far away. He however, Abraham, took the fire and the knife in his hand and both of them went together through this rotted city, which was to become new again, freed from rust, one sacrifice probably won't be enough to accomplish this, but better than nothing. Thus Isaac spoke to his father Abraham: My father! Abraham replied: Here I am my son. But it is not enough, it's not enough for the son to be there, a competent worker, who did not count, whoever counted anyway?, not he, okay, he didn't count either, only the father who, like any father, had learned to slaughter, it could be very useful to him, there always will be wars, here I am. My pleasure! And the son, who can't see a steel mill anywhere nor steel for that matter, he spoke: I see, here is fire and wood; but where is the iron to boil down, where is the product we are to produce, am I to be the product?, I have already been produced, after all, I've been brought here but—and we agreed on that—I was not to be destroyed, on the contrary, I am here to work, I finally received my draft call to work, I had to wait an eternity for it, Abraham replied, what's there for him to say?, my son, God will now get himself some sleep, no sheep, a sheep for the sacrifice. And here it is already, how pleasant, it has already been supplied, it will only have to be shorn, then we can kill it in peace and quiet. And thus they walked quietly together, father and son, who has the honor to play the sheep in the community-theatre performance I am presenting here. But there's no need for Abraham to do this, he would not go that far, these days you don't have to go that far for cigarettes, for work you do. No one has to do anything, no one has permission to do anything, there is no work, there is nothing to work on, what?, not yet, but soon?, I wouldn't hold my breath! There is no space for it, the space was promised, but it never arrived. It has been ordered but not delivered. It's at the neighbor no one knows. It would have come to us smoothly, but it won't come. This promise, unfortunately, must be taken back. Abraham may take his son back with him who has no idea at all what's going on and what had been decided about him and taken back again like the promise that people may work again, unfortunately also made by the father, the King, the husband. Work for the King is only a gratuity; he throws it to whatever he has to pay, that is to say, what the banks must pay for him; the people who campaigned so hard for him he throws as play money on the table. You however. How am I to know. You, however, King, King Oedipus, we'll still be hearing about him, having heard about him more than we wanted to hear, I'm afraid, you, King, now I'm asking you since we are on the topic: How come your superego got to be that huge, when did this happen, for a long time we didn't even notice, but now it can no longer be overlooked. Oh, I see, that isn't it, that is you. You always come yourself, you don't let yourself be represented.

The threat, that is you, I am now using you, I am playing you as the joker that's what people like me do, I am playing you as the joker, you are our threat and you made yourself come true! I realize this, but, my God, you are truly for real.

You freed yourself on and of your own personal responsi-bility, shook off your chains you were never put into and took the stage again. You are cast, so's the daughter, the son, the son-in-law, everyone's cast, by you and with you, though I would say, no, not I am saying this, that father and son add up to a brotherliness which, like any brotherliness will only bring trouble and conflict. Who generates the violence? The King, because he doesn't even have a brother? Brotherliness? Cut, and not only the role someone could take over. Outtakes, all of it? Take them all out? But I can't take them in, I have no room, I wouldn't know what to do with these people. They took shelter within themselves and that's taxing for everyone else, and that despite the tax cut. I am not making this up. It is true! You made it come true. I am self-employed, mostly manually, but don't know where my hands should go. I speak, therefore I also employ words whom I pay nothing but my attention. Call it minimum job security, without the security as to how it will go, which will be the next word to make sense, none of them have any. They are superfluous. My, our words are superfluous. The other words are talking now, they say something entirely different. They sharpened their perception like knives, even though they can't perceive anything because we don't explain it to them. They don't let themselves be displaced by anything anymore, not even by displacement itself; their Ego doesn't have to repress the sight of itself, it rather enjoys it, even though it has known itself for a long time, nothing gets replaced there anymore, now it's our turn to get displaced. Now you, King, do the talking, now you talk as all the others, who have also been

talking until now, but at least one could understand them.
The simple is simple, this, for example, is a simple sentence,
which even I can understand, that's why I sent it off without
further thought. So now the simple is the dominant power,
it has the power to destroy anyone who is not you. Okay, the
seer is leading the way, he lays the track. Could that be snow
where he is walking? At any rate, something that will vanish.
And if you want conclusive proofs of what was said, learn
the art of seership until you know it. By your son you shall
die? Why does God turn Abraham around here and make
him the sacrifice rather than Isaac? I don't understand.
Maybe the blind seers see it. They see two different things,
but there are also two seers. Both blind. All blind, blind all
of us.

I am not, I am and I am not, I must let go of my hopeful
inclination to speak and be listened to, brush it off, this inclination, which became hopeless long ago (yes, and while you
are at it, Ms. Author, brush him off too, that thinker, with
his *Wende* and *Kehre* and *being*, no, *beying*!, and what not,
which is missing in action, in that bloody act of translation).
Who are we anyway, who do we think we are to talk the way
we do? That's over. We are dying of our own failure, and
now we are despised. For what we were recently praised for,
got almost immortal, yes, the thinkers, yes, but also the
poets, the writers, pretty important too!, and this says one,
who will soon die, who no longer can foster any illusions.
None of her words will survive, already now none is alive
anymore. There one is twitching now, let's hit it, don't be

shy, but it's already quiet anyway. Now that you are here you've got the world in your hand, well at least the word, which wants to break out all the time, it wants to break away from me, from her, from that woman, do you know what she strives for? No, unfortunately we do not know, tell us, speak! Just let me leave this country and that's all she wrote, you won't even notice that I am missing, for I don't miss you either! It would be nice if someone would guide me, but I hold on to my stupid word and have only one free hand no one wants to take; I get carried away by my word, I carry on with it; I try to get away with it; yes, that too, but I am still getting on with it, though no longer getting it on with it, so I am getting out with it, no worries, I am not going anywhere, not with my word, I would not even want to spend my vacation with it, a time that is in principle worry free, no, we don't go and so it goes, soon I'll be gone, the King will be here, you've got him alright, you can get all upset about him or enjoy him, it doesn't matter, the main thing is that he is here, maybe he'll go before me? No, he isn't going to do that. Yes, you I mean, although I fear, it's really me who's meant by it: You are not afraid, Mr. King, of anything or anyone. You take the word by the hand and out of the House, you take the word out like a dog who keeps pulling at you, it wants to get going, the word wants to get away too, everything wants to get away, but no one yet knows whereto, at any rate, away from you, even though you control the ratings, what? I see, they keep falling. I'd only need one fall and that would be my downfall. Who's telling me that?, what does it tell me? That I'll die? I know that too.

Count no mortal happy till he has passed the final limit of his life secure from pain. My word!, (not really, guess whose), there's still a lot in store for me, I have the floor but my word is some place else, it says, it is with God, difficult to say anything against that. We cannot examine the word, because all private mail has been deleted, even exchanges that weren't private at all.

So we no longer have anything to say, that's our punishment and your joy. That makes you happy, doesn't it! Our epoch is over now, the ball point has perished long ago. Yours begins. We considered people to be our property, which had to listen to us, now: painful disappointment. Nobody listened. All that time no one! So, and now I missed the TV news to boot. Thus, unfortunately, I can't tell you what you should do. Because I don't know myself, even though I've always known before. And that stupid word is pulling me again, it almost tears my arm out of its socket. It found another one, on the playground over there, with whom it wants to chat a bit. As for me, I am totally unsuited for such entertainment, I have to get mine from little silver discs. So why don't you entertain us, you ask. I'd like to, but I must live up to my responsibility, a popular joke of lazy folks, the responsibility that must finally be followed by a response. I don't have it. But I have been given it frequently: hypocrite is the response. Here, on that banner, meant for me, it is written, loud and clear, and here too. Okay, I admit: Nothing is true. True? Might people's misery have become too big? No, no worries, they'll grow into it. The King is to blame for the city's demise, just because he has come and now he is here. Because he is who he is. The King is guilty, now we know it. He committed the outrageous transgression of letting himself be voted King by us. So now he is responsible. He is deep into debt. He's got such riches in debts that none is left. Now we could use a real miracle. We might be in for quite an experience. It always happens in the now. Everything falls silent, the word is out of sight and sniffs at the ass of another one, then it walks away, fairly unimpressed. It would recognize another word anytime, anywhere, but what would that bring us? It would be nice if two words that understand each other well, could also meet each other again. It might have even happened occasionally, I just didn't notice. Not a single voice raised in contradiction. The die is cast. I accuse. I collect my gathered accusations which are falling from the altar I laid myself down on, it's quite a lot!, but I am the last thing God would want, a boy might have a chance, even though he is not a football coach, no educator, priest or bishop, he is above that, I mean, he outranks all of them. But God certainly does not want me, even though I once adored him so much, no one wants me the way I look now, the way it looks, no one wants me now, old age is a massacre which was also done to me, I've already said it more often than it did me any good, otherwise it might have overlooked me, the one that was done to me, here, in this column, in this word, which I don't know because it is anonymous, you can also read it, but you already knew it anyway, exactly the way it is written here. I count my accusations. Even when I send them to you, some are returned as undeliverable, delivery refused. The sacrifice did not take place, it was not accepted, the sacrifice has a crisis, the crisis wants the sacrifice, no, it would like a different sacrifice, no, not that one either. But here they come already—millions of delicious victims, come on in! knife and fork placed in their backs, how is one to decide? They all look okay, we are already searching for recipes for sauces. Are they all coming then?, are all of you coming, so that the unity of this seriously injured community can be established again? Chaos. Horror. No golden thread to be found anymore, not even one for opening the package, but there doesn't have to be one, you won't like what's inside. Someone sacrifices this, another that, the third one himself, the forth gets dragged there by his father, but not even that one gets accepted. Thousands more victims are already waiting behind the barrier, maybe a better one will be among those.

Must we offer sacrifices to the King, because God doesn't want them? Everywhere the same drive, the same death, the same hate, the same compulsion, the same illusion that in this country, which is nominally united, if only with itself, that there could be real unity in this country. Sighing deeply, the country raises her hand, she volunteers, but the sign could also mean something else entirely. Others should follow, others should follow her. She shakes me, she shakes the victim, because it is losing so much blood that flows blackly down from the wound on the thigh, wounds instead of eyes, wherever. What are the news saying, this time I definitely will watch them, they will be the latest, the old ones I missed will surely look old by comparison, and expire in front of my eyes, they say: Old resentments, old hatred—which should actually be spread out among all of you, so everyone can get something out of them, says this man—are directed at one single individual, whom I unfortunately cannot get here for you in person to tell you himself, they are directed at the King who anyone could be, but is not, you didn't know that, huh? The King is he, it's him alright, and now he should be the one everything flows into, hopes first, they'll soon be checked off, but the feelings of hate, resentment, how about those? Directed at him, the King, the one and only, the reconciling sacrifice. Pay special attention to the word reconciling. Though it is not the one that broke away from me, I never had anything to do with reconciliation, it is an entirely new word that came to me because my old one couldn't take it with me any longer.

Please come back to me, dear word, or do I first have to call an angel? Here he is, I didn't even have to call, he's been here the whole time! So there the Angel of the LORD of Heaven calls somebody, cursing the provider, because he hasn't yet put up a tower or whatever he wanted to provide us with, first of all for a minimum rate so that we too can talk to anyone and listen to no one, it wouldn't be worth it anyway, who'd want to talk to God, the distance is too far, the rate is coming to get us now, but we have gotten much further, the angel dialed this number so that the word can spread, he looks at the display to check whether he'd dialed the right number since no one's picking up the phone. Come on now, how long does he want to wait, before he gets a connection. Apparently, it wants to make itself at home here, because it won't get higher up, the word which is with God, no, it is not, the word had an accident, it can't get anywhere, it stays and it is also gone again. Whatever.

Skyping won't work in this case, what's there to see anyway? There is nothing there, only desolation. No factories. No mines. No work. No works. Someone spoke to us, we did not hear it, but someone must have said it: Away with it, away with the word, with every word, we'd rather pick a different word, so that we can lose it too, we lost everything, now we are also running out of words, they are running off to where there still is room for conversation. Please take your place on the sacrificial rock, make yourself comfortable, I am just getting the knife: Abraham! Abraham! And he answers, as said before, not by me, so it is correct: I am here. Just a moment, I can't see exactly who that even is, but he seems to be here. My word has gone crazy, probably because it thought it lost me, but I am not at a loss for words and the word speaks: Do not lay your hand on the boy or do anything to him, for now I know that you fear God, seeing you have not withheld your son, your only son, for my sake!

★ ★ ★

Okay, all of you, one more time out with me for the curtain call:

David Cay Johnston, *The Making of Donald Trump*

Sophocles, *Oedipus the King*

René Girard, *Violence and the Sacred*

Martin Heidegger, as always, this time the *Black Notebooks*

And other stuff, I can't remember everything, newspaper articles, things like that.

David Graeber, *Debt*

Sigmund Freud, *The Dissolution of the Oedipus Complex*

The following is an excerpt from Jelinek's program note for the Vienna Burgtheater's production of her new play *Schwarzwasser* (*Waste Water*) that premiered in January 2020 with great success at the Vienna Akademietheater. It is her instant response to the so-called Ibiza-affair or Ibiza-gate, news of which broke in May 2019. It involved and quickly forced the resignation of Austria's deputy chancellor and leader of the far-right Freedom Party (FPÖ), Heinz Christian Strache, whose corrupt strategies evoke those of Donald Trump. As the *Guardian* reported:

> [T]wo German media outlets published a video that shows the deputy chancellor, talking to an unidentified woman purporting to be the niece of a Russian oligarch at a luxury resort in Ibiza. When the woman expresses an interest in gaining control of the country's largest-circulation tabloid, *Kronen Zeitung,* Strache suggests he could offer lucrative public contracts in exchange for campaign support.[1]

---

1 Philip Oltermann, "Austria's 'Ibiza Scandal': What Happened and Why Does It Matter?" *Guradian*, May 20, 2019. Available at: http://bit.ly/-2TFJwjL (last accessed on March 11, 2020).

In her program note, Jelinek introduces her new play in the context of the trivializing of politics in many countries, with the US president as the foremost example. The excerpt also illuminates her understanding and use of the stage and the role of theater in political discourses.

Gitta Honegger

My theater texts are primarily texts for speaking (and also texts for reading), a way of speaking, however, that is exhibited, so to speak, in order to get a collective response. As in Greek theater, I put my figures on cothurns, but actually they are not figures, it is my speaking itself that speaks and creates figures in the process, they should speak me, so to speak (not just in place of me). I speak very little privately, because I rarely go out among people. Thus I borrow my speaking from the mouth of the actor, perhaps so that what I say becomes finally important. Maybe it is a kind of free speech loan. I can't derive any claims from it. And what I say can be revoked any time by the audience. But since the reception is collective, the individual doesn't get to me with his approval or rejection.

Of course I believe that the theater is allowed to do anything and it really can do most of it. What's been said (and even done) spills out into reality, whose solid ground gets flooded by it. For example, at present, I see the new populist leaders everywhere, who go for the stage of the public sphere, reclaim it for themselves, thus reducing the Dionysian element of the festival to media size, so that they are able to lift it and seize it. The trivializing of politics, as it is currently practiced in many countries: most of all, I see it in the USA, that is, by Trump who, with his own method of counterfeiting reality, practices a process of banalizing and re-ideologizing of politics, where this fact isn't the worst of it, but, rather, that everything helps him, as all new leaders, including everything that is directed against him and perhaps, most of all, the latter. They feed themselves with everything and whip up their followers to a false union and unity. I see this crisis of the sacrificial cult, as described by Girard. The tragedy, which outside the theater is wrought by the populists' speeches, literally throws the listeners back to the violence that is the origin of the festival. The Dionysian element is evoked by the new chorus and at the same time parodied by the audience chanting the campaign speeches of the ludicrous liar and clown Donald Trump, until the chorus melts into one single baiting crowd, which no longer allows for sublimation and catharsis (e.g. at the campaign events back then against Hillary Clinton: "Lock her up, lock her up!" and similar, thrown, puked-out chunks that are immediately picked up and chanted by the mob as a profanation of the sacred chorus). The old means of the theater that are carried on in multiple ways (also by me, yes, I always like to pick some) are thus reflected in populist politics, which I see, as I said, on the march everywhere, that is in the direct, trivial and ultimately banal baiting speech, which also creates a collective, albeit not united in cult or art, but in darker energies like envy or hate of those different kinds of people, strangers, the unassimilated. I would like to see the theater as the opposite to a propaganda instrument (as the Nazis, for example, accomplished with the spin they put on their productions of classical dramas to push their politics through). The theater should be immune against such attempts and, as far as I can see, it does become more and more open-minded and diverse as the more simple-minded the public is kept. Not Austria (a pope once called it that) is an island of the blessed; the theater is. I, too, can take a seat there.

Elfriede Jelinek

THE CORONATION OF KING TRUMP

During the editing process with the publisher of this book, the outbreak of Covid-19, the coronavirus disease in the US, was first reported. Having internalized Elfriede Jelinek's linguistic strategies as her longtime translator, the name of the virus merged with the fulfillment of Trump's royal dream turned nightmare. In the meantime, the coronation of the King as she envisioned him the morning after his ominous election has actually begun and now the nation and the world suffers through the disease with no end in sight.